AUBAMEYANG

MATT AND TOM OLDFIELD

ULTIMATE FOOTBALL HEROES

AUBAMEYANG

FROM THE PLAYGROUND
TO THE PITCH

DINO

First published by Dino Books in 2019,
an imprint of Bonnier Books UK,
The Plaza,
535 Kings Road,
London SW10 0SZ

@dinobooks
@footieheroesbks
www.heroesfootball.com
www.bonnierbooks.co.uk

Design and typesetting by www.envydesign.co.uk

Paperback ISBN: 978 1 78946 119 0
E-book ISBN: 978 1 78946 182 4

British Library Cataloguing-in-Publication Data:
A catalogue record for this book is available from the British Library.

Printed and bound in Great Britain by Clays Ltd, Elcograf S.p.A.

1 3 5 7 9 10 8 6 4 2

For Iona, Katie, Ian, Naomi, Barny, Beckie,
Rob and Dion Dublin

ULTIMATE FOOTBALL HEROES

Matt Oldfield is an accomplished writer and the editor-in-chief of football review site *Of Pitch & Page*. Tom Oldfield is a freelance sports writer and the author of biographies on Cristiano Ronaldo, Arsène Wenger and Rafael Nadal.

Cover illustration by Dan Leydon.
To learn more about Dan visit danleydon.com
To purchase his artwork visit etsy.com/shop/footynews
Or just follow him on Twitter @danleydon

TABLE OF CONTENTS

ACKNOWLEDGEMENTS

First of all, I'd like to thank Bonnier Books UK – and particularly my editor Laura Pollard – for supporting me throughout and running the ever-expanding UFH ship so smoothly. Writing stories for the next generation of football fans is both an honour and a pleasure.

I wouldn't be doing this if it wasn't for my brother Tom. I owe him so much and I'm very grateful for his belief in me as an author. I feel like Robin setting out on a solo career after a great partnership with Batman. I hope I do him (Tom, not Batman) justice with these new books.

Next up, I want to thank my friends for keeping me sane during long hours in front of the laptop.

Pang, Will, Mills, Doug, John, Charlie – the laughs and the cups of coffee are always appreciated.

I've already thanked my brother but I'm also very grateful to the rest of my family, especially Melissa, Noah and of course Mum and Dad. To my parents, I owe my biggest passions: football and books. They're a real inspiration for everything I do.

Finally, I couldn't have done this without Iona's encouragement and understanding during long, work-filled weekends. Much love to you.

CHAPTER 1

AUBA'S ARSENAL GOLDEN BOOT

12 May 2019, Turf Moor Stadium

It was the last day of the Premier League season, and Arsenal were determined to end on a high, aiming for a big win away at Burnley. Unless they thrashed The Clarets by seven or eight goals, the Gunners would finish fifth, just outside of the Champions League places.

'Hey, it's not over until it's over!' Pierre-Emerick told his teammates before kick-off.

Arsenal's main man was on a goalscoring mission. He was raring to return to the Champions League, plus he really wanted to win the Golden Boot. He had done it in Germany at Borussia Dortmund, and now he wanted to do it in England too.

With one game to go, Pierre-Emerick was on twenty Premier League goals for the season. That put him joint second in the race, tied with Liverpool's Sadio Mané and Manchester City's Sergio Agüero. Only Mohamed Salah had scored more – two more.

'No problem, I'll win it with a hat-trick then!' Pierre-Emerick discussed with his partner in attack and best friend, Alexandre Lacazette. Together at Arsenal, 'Auba' and 'Laca' had formed one of the most entertaining and effective strikeforces in European football.

Pierre-Emerick said it with a smile on his face, as always, but when it came to scoring goals, he was 100 per cent serious. Only three days earlier, he had scored a hat-trick against Valencia in the Europa League semi-final. There was no reason why he couldn't do that again for Arsenal.

Playing up front on his own, Pierre-Emerick was full of energy and clever movement. In the fourth minute, he darted away from his marker and headed Henrikh Mkhitaryan's cross goalwards. The

Burnley keeper was beaten but the ball bounced back off the post.

So close to the perfect start! But Pierre-Emerick didn't stand there with his hands on his head, thinking about all the 'what if's. Instead, he ran back into position, hoping for another chance, just like his old Dortmund teammate Robert Lewandowski had taught him:

'If I do miss one, I just make sure that I score the next one.'

All Pierre-Emerick needed was one good pass and his pace would do the rest…

Shkodran Mustafi played a long ball over the top and *ZOOM!* he was off, sprinting into the Burnley box. From wide on the right, Pierre-Emerick went for goal. *BANG!* His shot was heading for the top corner, but this time, the keeper saved it.

'Arghhhhhhhhh!' the Arsenal supporters sighed. They were right behind Auba in his quest for the Golden Boot.

It was surely only a matter of time before Pierre-Emerick scored. Early in the second half the Burnley centre-back, Ben Mee, lost control of the ball near the halfway line. Big mistake! Pierre-Emerick pounced and raced away towards goal, with three defenders trailing behind. He was one-on-one with the keeper now, one of his favourite games to play. With lots of hard work in training, Pierre-Emerick had become one of the world's best at it.

Which side would he shoot? Right, left, or maybe even down the middle, through Burnley goalkeeper Tom Heaton's legs? Pierre-Emerick waited for the keeper to make the first move and then coolly slotted the ball just past his outstretched left arm. *1–0!*

Goooooooooooooooooooooaaaaaaaaaaaaaaaaaallllllllllll llllllllllllllll!!!!!!!!!!!!!!!!!!!!!

He had scored Goal Number Twenty-One! There was no way he was going to miss a golden chance like that to celebrate. He jogged past the Arsenal fans behind the goal, proudly patting the club badge on his shirt. He loved being their star striker, following in the footsteps of his childhood hero, Thierry Henry.

So, how many more could Auba score? As Alex Iwobi chipped a cross from the left, Pierre-Emerick made a run in behind the Burnley left-back. The ball flew just over Charlie Taylor's head and dropped down dangerously, in front of Pierre-Emerick's golden right boot. *BANG!* He struck it sweetly on the volley into the far corner of the net.

Goooooooooooooooooooaaaaaaaaaaaaaaaalllllllllllll llllllllllllll!!!!!!!!!!!!!!!!!!!

Number Twenty-Two! It was a beautiful finish, one that Pierre-Emerick had been practising ever since childhood, when he would watch videos with his grandad of Real Madrid's Hugo Sánchez. To pull it off in the Premier League, though – that was very special indeed.

For once, there were no somersault celebrations or handshakes with Laca. Pierre-Emerick thanked Alex for the assist and then went hunting for his hat-trick goal.

He cut inside one Burnley centre-back, but the other came across to clear. *Nearly!*

Another cross from Alex flew just over his head. *Nearly!*

Then, there was the best chance of them all. As

Mkhi raced down the right wing, he knew exactly where his old Dortmund teammate would be in the middle. He curled a perfect pass towards him, but somehow Pierre-Emerick poked it wide.

He couldn't believe it – how had he missed *that*? Oh well, there were still twenty minutes left…

Unfortunately, Auba's third goal never arrived. He finished with twenty-two goals for the season, and so did Liverpool's Mohamed Salah *and* Sadio Mané. All three of them would have to share the Premier League Golden Boot.

'Three Africans together!' Pierre-Emerick joked. He was happy, at least this time, to share the award with two players he really admired.

'Next season, though, that prize will be all mine!' he declared.

Although he loved to laugh and entertain, his journey to the top hadn't always been easy. There had been difficult times in Italy, and back home in France too. But with hard work and determination, he had developed into one of the greatest goalscorers on the planet. And Arsenal's star striker was only getting started.

CHAPTER 2

SON OF A LAVAL LEGEND

For many football-mad kids, Saturdays are all about going to the park for a fun kickaround with friends and family. However, it was a little different for Pierre-Emerick. Why? Because his dad was a real professional footballer!

Pierre 'Yaya' Aubameyang was a defensive midfielder for Stade Lavallois, a club in north-west France who played in the French First Division, Ligue 1. That's right, every week, Pierre-Emerick's dad got to compete against some of the best players on the planet! Roger Milla, Glenn Hoddle, Eric Cantona, George Weah…

He was the coolest dad ever and, of course, he was Pierre-Emerick's favourite footballer.

'And he's an *international* too!' the boy boasted proudly to his friends at school. He was only five years old, but he had practised that word over and over until he could say it perfectly.

Pierre-Emerick's dad came from Gabon, a small nation on the west coast of Africa. He was one of The Panthers' most experienced stars and he had just helped them reach the 1994 African Cup of Nations. 'Yaya' had lived in Gabon until he moved to France to play football and start a family. Pierre-Emerick was born in Laval, but his dad loved telling him stories about his homeland.

'One day, I'll take you there!' Yaya promised his son.

Pierre-Emerick nodded eagerly, but what he wanted most of all was for his dad to teach him all his awesome football skills. They often practised together on the big pitch near their house. They were usually the only people around. Laval was a small, rural town, more famous for its cows than its footballers. But Pierre-Emerick was determined to change that.

'What a shot, son!' His dad clapped and cheered as the ball whizzed right past him and between the goal posts. 'You're going to be a star striker when you're older, I can tell!'

Pierre-Emerick grinned widely; that was the plan. He was going to become a Laval legend just like his dad – only he'd score a lot more goals!

Pierre-Emerick certainly had the perfect preparation for life as a famous footballer. He spent most Saturdays watching Yaya and his Laval teammates playing at the Stade Francis Le Basser, or at even bigger stadiums around France. He loved everything about the game: the atmosphere, the colours, the songs, but most of all, he loved the goals and the celebrations.

'Woah, did you see that? Sooooo cool!'

However, like most five-year-olds, Pierre-Emerick found it hard to sit still for a full football match, even when his own dad was out there on the pitch. Watching was just nowhere near as fun as actually playing. As soon as he saw a bit of skill that he really liked, Pierre-Emerick couldn't help himself; he had to try it out.

'Hey, has anyone got a football?' he would ask his friends, most of whom were the kids of other Stade Lavallois stars.

If someone said yes, brilliant! But if not, they would find something else to kick around instead – a can, a stone, even a scrunched-up ball of paper. And that would keep them busy until... half-time!

Pierre-Emerick loved half-time – it was his favourite part of the whole football match. That's because when Laval were at home, the players' kids were sometimes allowed to go out onto the pitch and play.

'Come on, let's go!' they'd shout excitedly as they raced into the penalty area to strike as many shots as they could before the second half started.

At half-time, the Stade Francis Le Basser was never as loud as it was while the real game was going on, but that didn't matter because Pierre-Emerick had a strong imagination. In his head, he could hear

the crowd roar as he stepped up to take the final
spot-kick in the French Cup Final. This was his big
moment – could he become the Laval hero? After a
really long run-up, he pulled back his right leg and
fired the ball towards the bottom corner...

*Goooooooooooooooooooaaaaaaaaaaaaaaaalllllllllllll
llllllllllllll!!!!!!!!!!!!!!!!!!!*

CHAPTER 3

SOMERSAULTS LIKE SÁNCHEZ

*Gooooooooooooooooooooaaaaaaaaaaaaaaaalllllllllllllllll
lllllllll!!!!!!!!!!!!!!!!!!!!!*

*Gooooooooooooooooooooaaaaaaaaaaaaaaaalllllllllllllllll
lllllllll!!!!!!!!!!!!!!!!!!!!!*

*Gooooooooooooooooooooaaaaaaaaaaaaaaaalllllllllllllllll
lllllllll!!!!!!!!!!!!!!!!!!!!!*

Pierre-Emerick couldn't get enough of that scoring
feeling. Whenever the ball crossed the goal line and
nestled in the back of the net, he just wanted to
celebrate like crazy. At first, he would leap high into
the air or throw himself across the grass, but then he
discovered something much more spectacular: the
somersault.

And it was all thanks to a Mexican striker called Hugo Sánchez. Between 1985 and 1992, Sánchez starred for Real Madrid, Pierre-Emerick's grandfather's favourite team. Football really did run deep in Pierre-Emerick's far-flung family. While his dad was from Gabon, his mum, Margarita, was from Spain. And her father was from Ávila, a city only 120 kilometres away from Madrid.

'You'll be a Real fan too!' his grandfather had decided as soon as he was born. To make 100 per cent sure, he educated Pierre-Emerick in two very important ways:

1) by telling lots of long football stories
2) by showing him videos of the club's greatest moments.

It didn't take long at all for Pierre-Emerick to fall in love with 'The Whites'. The club had so much history and so many brilliant players. Sánchez, however, was definitely his favourite. The Mexican forward only seemed to score really great goals: free kicks, cheeky chips, long-range rockets, diving headers, acrobatic volleys and best of all, overhead kicks.

'Here we go, this is the best of the bunch!' his grandfather said, pointing enthusiastically as if it was the first time that he'd seen it, rather than the five hundredth. '*La perfecta chilena!*'

'What does that mean, Grandpa?'

'The perfect bicycle kick! Trust me, it's the greatest goal I've ever seen.'

They watched in silence as the cross came in from the left wing. It was going to land behind Sánchez, so he stepped back and then jumped up athletically with his back to goal. *BANG!* His left foot struck the ball beautifully – his technique was perfect. It flew past the keeper and into the top corner.

Gooooooooooooooooooooaaaaaaaaaaaaaaaalllllllllllll llllllllllllll!!!!!!!!!!!!!!!!!!!

'Honestly, I've never heard a cheer like it,' his grandfather continued, smiling at the memory. 'The supporters were up on their feet clapping for ages. The Real fans *and* the Logroñés fans together – that's how special it was!'

'Wow, what a *beauty*!' Pierre-Emerick cheered in awe. 'That was the best thing I've ever seen! Can we watch it again?'

But the spectacle of great goals was only half the fun of his new favourite player. Because when Sánchez scored, he really knew how to celebrate in style.

One time, he sat down on the grass and lifted up his scoring boot.

Another time, he sank to his knees and threw his arms up triumphantly.

But his most famous celebration of all was the somersault. Sánchez made it look so easy and so exciting. He threw his hands down, flipped his body in mid-air and then landed on his feet like a proper gymnast, punching the air while the crowd went wild.

'I've changed my mind,' Pierre-Emerick screamed at the TV screen, '*THAT* is the best thing I've ever seen!'

Yes, that was exactly the kind of player that he wanted to be when he was older – successful but also stylish, effective and entertaining.

Sánchez had managed to win five La Liga titles *and* the UEFA Cup at Real Madrid. He was a club legend and the greatest Mexican player of all time. Pierre-Emerick wanted the glory of winning top trophies, but he also wanted the fame of being a fun footballer. If Sánchez could be both, then so could he.

'Thanks Grandpa, I need to go and practise now!' he said, jumping off the sofa.

'Won't you need your football for that?' his grandfather asked. Pierre-Emerick had left it behind in the living room.

'No, I'm not practising my skills today,' he explained. 'I'm practising my somersaults!'

CHAPTER 4

SHINING STRAIGHT AWAY

Usually, kids had to be six years old before they could join the local junior football team, ASL L'Huisserie. Pierre-Emerick, however, was allowed to start at the age of five. By then, he had already been badgering his dad for over a year.

'Pleeeeeeeeaaaaaaase! I must be old enough now...'

When, at last, Pierre asked if his son could play, the coach Alain Guinoiseau thought to himself:

'Why not? If he's anything like his father, the boy's going to be brilliant!'

And he was right about that. From his very first touch of the football, Pierre-Emerick stood out from the rest of his new teammates. There were several reasons for that:

1) His speed

Wow, Guinoiseau had never seen anyone so fast at such a young age! One second, the kids would all be battling for the ball in the middle of the field and the next, *ZOOM!* Pierre-Emerick would break away, leaving everyone else trailing a long way behind. In their warm-up runs, he was always miles ahead at the front. It was like he had a superpower, or two turbo engines hidden in his football boots.

'Maybe he should be a sprinter instead?' the L'Huisserie coach wondered at first.

2) His goals

But soon Guinoiseau decided: 'No, this boy is born to be a footballer!'

Whenever he got the ball, Pierre-Emerick only had one thing on his mind – scoring a goal. It was all he wanted to do. The coach saw the determined look on his face as he dribbled forward as fast as he could, followed by the look of delight when he succeeded in beating the keeper.

Goooooooooooooooooooooaaaaaaaaaaaaaaaaaallllllllllll lllllllllllllll!!!!!!!!!!!!!!!!!!!!!

The other L'Huisserie players enjoyed playing football, but Pierre-Emerick loved it more than anything in the whole wide world.

3) His goal celebrations

There were lots of goals, and that meant lots of celebrations. Luckily, Pierre-Emerick had been practising his Sánchez somersaults, and this was the perfect opportunity for him to show them off.

'Watch this!' he called out and then flipped his body through the air, before landing on his feet again.

It was as if Pierre-Emerick was a proper superstar already! Guinoiseau could easily picture him entertaining thousands of fans in years to come.

'Yes, he's going to be huge!'

*

For now, Pierre-Emerick was just performing in

front of friends and family, but that was enough
of an audience. His dad came to watch him play
for L'Huisserie whenever he could, and so did his
grandfather.

'Go on, Pierre-Emerick!' they cheered him on from
the sidelines.

Right, time to shine! When he raced towards goal,
the opposition defenders had no chance. Even if they
had a head start, *ZOOM!* Pierre-Emerick would fly
past them in a flash, fully focused on his target:

*Goooooooooooooooooooaaaaaaaaaaaaaaaalllllllllllll
llllllllllllll!!!!!!!!!!!!!!!!!!!*

'YES!' It was the best feeling in the world, and
Pierre-Emerick was always hungry for more. With
his coach's help, he kept improving all the time, and
learning new ways to fire L'Huisserie to victory. But
he didn't just want to score lots of goals; he wanted
to score lots of *GREAT* goals, just like his Real Madrid
hero, Sánchez.

One game, a cross came into the box and it was
going to land behind Pierre-Emerick.

'This is my chance!' he thought excitedly. He had

been waiting ages for an opportunity like this.

So he stepped back and then jumped up athletically with his back to the goal. *BANG!* His right foot struck the ball beautifully – his technique was perfect. It flew past the keeper and into the top corner.

Goooooooooooooooooooooaaaaaaaaaaaaaaaaalllllllllllll lllllllllllllll!!!!!!!!!!!!!!!!!!

'YEEEEESSSSSS!' What an unforgettable moment! He had scored with a brilliant bicycle kick that even Sánchez himself would have been proud of. Not as proud as Pierre-Emerick's grandfather, however.

'That's the new greatest goal I've ever seen!' he shouted, as a big grin spread across his face.

CHAPTER 5

BEDROOM BERNABÉU

'Clarence Seedorf finds Aubameyang with a perfect pass, and he's off, racing past the Barcelona defence and into the penalty area! He's now one on one with the keeper... Can Real Madrid's star striker score the winning goal in the very last minute of the match?'

Pierre-Emerick's commentary stopped as he steadied himself to take the all-important shot. He took a deep breath to slow down his racing heartbeat, and then a quick look up at the target to pick his spot.

'You can do this!' he whispered to himself.

His club was counting on him – his teammates, his coaches, and all the fans (toys) who filled the famous

Bernabéu stadium (his bedroom). He was Real Madrid's new Number 9 – that's what it said on the back of his white football shirt, a birthday gift from his grandparents.

Pierre-Emerick pulled back his right leg and aimed the small, soft football towards the bottom right corner of the net (the gap between his bed and the cupboard).

'That's a fierce strike from Aubameyang but can Ruud Hesp dive down quickly enough to keep it out?' the commentary continued. 'No!'

His bedroom football dramas always ended the same way:

'*Goooooooaaaaaaalllllllllll!*' cried Pierre-Emerick the TV commentator,

'*Goooooooaaaaaaalllllllllll!*' cried Pierre-Emerick, acting the part of all the Real Madrid supporters in one,

'*Goooooooaaaaaaalllllllllll!*' cried Pierre-Emerick the Real Madrid manager, and '*Goooooooaaaaaaalllllllllll!*' cried Pierre-Emerick, Real Madrid's star striker.

There wasn't enough space in his bedroom for

his usual somersault celebration, so he took a bow instead.

'Aubameyang is the Real Madrid hero – what composure under pressure! Can anyone stop this wonderkid?'

At the final whistle, he sank to his knees and punched the air. The magnificent noise of the crowd made him shiver with excitement.

HALA MADRID! HALA MADRID!

After hugging his teammates, Raúl and Roberto Carlos, and then swapping shirts with Rivaldo, it was time for his post-match interview. He put on a deep voice for this part:

'So, Pierre-Emerick how does it feel to score the winning goal in your first *El Clásico*?'

'It really is a dream come true for me. It's great to score the winning goal, but the result is the most important thing. I'd like to thank my manager for believing in me, my teammates, and everyone else at the club. I—'

Suddenly, Pierre-Emerick's moment of fame was interrupted by a strange, muffled noise coming from

out in the hallway. What was it? It sounded like…
like someone trying their hardest not to giggle. Uh
oh, he had a larger audience than he had realised.

'Hey, go away!' Pierre-Emerick called out as he
stormed over to open his bedroom door.

His older half-brothers, Catilina and Willy, had
been standing outside the whole time, with their
ears pressed against the door. They had heard every
embarrassing word of Pierre-Emerick's football fairy
tale. And now they were rolling around on the floor,
laughing their heads off.

'Sorry, I didn't realise we were living with
Aubameyang, Real Madrid's star striker!'

'That was *some* story, bro – they should really
make a TV series about you!'

'Willy's right: "what composure under pressure" –
where did you even learn that phrase?'

With each joke aimed at him, Pierre-Emerick's
face grew redder and redder. Finally, he shouted,
'I said GO AWAY!' and then slammed the door
behind him. Sadly, even that didn't stop his brothers
straight away.

'Hey, we're only teasing, mate. Say hi to Seedorf from me!'

'And Roberto Carlos! Can we come and play at the Bernabéu too one day?'

At first, Pierre-Emerick sat there on his bed in silence, feeling really, really silly. Why hadn't he checked to make sure the coast was clear? What if Catilina and Willy told his friends about his little performance? The school playground would be a nightmare for weeks!

But once he had calmed down a little, he changed his mind. Maybe the situation wasn't so bad, after all. His brothers were just joking around; they wouldn't be that mean.

'Besides, who cares what they think?' he decided. 'They won't be laughing at me anymore when I make my football dream come true!'

CHAPTER 6

THE ULTIMATE FOOTBALL HERO

First, there was his dad, then Hugo Sánchez and his somersaults, but by 2002, Pierre-Emerick had found his ultimate football hero – Ronaldo Luís Nazário de Lima.

'You can call me Ronaldo from now on!' he told his teammates at training.

Pierre-Emerick had never seen anyone quite like Ronaldo, not even George Weah or Thierry Henry. Usually, strikers were either small and quick, or big and powerful. But Brazil's Number 9 had it all: speed, strength, skill, plus a rocket of a shot. And like Sánchez, Ronaldo still offered that magical mix of talent and entertainment. Pierre-Emerick was mesmerised.

'Did you see his strike against Turkey? On the volley too!'

He watched every minute of every match that Ronaldo played at the 2002 World Cup. Then he rewatched all his goals another twenty times each: the tap-ins against China and Costa Rica, the side-foot finish through the Belgium goalkeeper's legs and the dribble and toe-poke to take Brazil into the World Cup Final.

'Yeah, but the goalie definitely should have saved that one!' his friends tried to argue, but Pierre-Emerick, of course, disagreed. He wouldn't hear a bad word said about his ultimate football hero.

'No, because Ronaldo surprised him by shooting early. Trust me, he's a genius!'

Ronaldo was on a roll, but what would he do in the World Cup Final, the biggest game of all? Pierre-Emerick had been nine years old for the 1998 final between Brazil and France. That day, he had cheered for his homeland as Zidane became the hero instead, with two brilliant headers.

This time, though, it was Ronaldo's turn. First, he pounced on a mistake by the Germany goalkeeper, Oliver Kahn. *1–0!*

'Yes! RONALDO, RONALDO!' Pierre-Emerick cheered from the sofa.

Then, two minutes later, the Brazilian scored again in that same bottom corner. *2–0!*

'What a genius!' Pierre-Emerick declared, and no-one in his family could disagree with that.

His love for his ultimate football hero was about to get even stronger too.

'Have you heard the news, Grandpa?' Pierre-Emerick asked excitedly later that summer. 'Ronaldo has signed for Real Madrid!'

They couldn't wait to see their favourite team's new star striker in action. Ronaldo missed the first few matches of the new Spanish league season, but he was on the bench for the home game against Alavés.

'He's going to come on and score,' Pierre-Emerick predicted, 'I just know it!'

He was right. With thirty minutes to go, Real were winning 2–1 and the fans were crying out for *El Fenómeno*. One fan watching in France was especially excited.

'*Finally* – here he comes!' Pierre-Emerick cheered.

Wearing the Number 11 shirt, Ronaldo ran on to replace Javier Portillo in attack. And just one minute later, his name was already on the scoresheet.

Robert Carlos's cross from the left floated over the heads of the Alavés centre-backs, and Ronaldo chested the ball down beautifully.

'Go on – shoot!'

The Brazilian only had the keeper left to beat, just like Pierre-Emerick in his bedroom Bernabeu. What would he do next? Dribble around him? Slide it through his legs?

No, instead, Ronaldo decided to hit his shot down into the grass, and it bounced up over the keeper's outstretched arms and into the top corner. *3–1!*

What a clever finish! Pierre-Emerick would be practising that one for weeks, first in the park with his friends and then on the pitch for his football team.

But Ronaldo wasn't done yet. Fifteen minutes later, he collected a pass from Steve McManaman and curled the ball around the keeper and then just past the sliding legs of two desperate Alavés defenders on the goal line. *5–1!*

'How did he *do* that?' The accuracy was astounding!

Ronaldo soon had a chance to complete his hat-trick, but this time, his shot flew well wide of the post.

Pierre-Emerick was shocked into silence, but his grandfather laughed. 'See, he *is* human, after all!'

Ronaldo helped Real Madrid win the Spanish League title in his very first season at the club. But over in France, his biggest fan was having a few little troubles of his own.

CHAPTER 7

ALWAYS ON
THE MOVE

'Hey, what's wrong?' Yaya asked as his son trudged off the Rouen training pitch towards him.

Pierre-Emerick wasn't in the mood for an explanation. After years of finding football the most fun thing in the world, it had suddenly become really frustrating.

There were two main reasons for that. Firstly, despite still only being fifteen years old, he was now playing for his fourth football club. He had spent a year at Nice in between spells at L'Huissierie, before joining his local professional team, Stade Lavallois, and then Rouen.

That was an awful lot of moving around and

making new friends. Every football club was
so different – the atmosphere, the tactics, the
coaching, and the characters in the dressing room.
Sometimes, it took Pierre-Emerick time to settle
in and feel comfortable being his shiny, superstar,
somersaulting self. And this time, the move hadn't
even been his choice; his dad had signed for
Rouen's senior team and so he'd had to follow.

'Sorry, son,' Yaya had said as they packed up their
things and travelled nearly 200 miles to their new
home, 'but you'll need to get used to this lifestyle
if you want to be a professional footballer when
you're older.'

But *was* that what Pierre-Emerick still wanted –
to bounce from one club to the next, always on the
move? For the first time in his life, he wasn't so sure.

However, that wasn't only because of all the
moving around. There was another reason for Pierre-
Emerick's unhappiness.

For years, he had been the fastest player around.
Yes, he was good at shooting too, but speed had
always been his superpower. It had helped him win

so many football matches, often pretty much on his own. He was used to hearing opposition defenders shout to each other, 'Watch out for the quick guy on the wing!'

Suddenly, however, that wasn't true anymore. It had all started with some pain in his knees. At first, he had tried to play on, but in the end, he'd had to hobble off the field.

'Don't worry, this sort of injury happens to all young players,' his dad reassured him. 'With a bit of rest, you'll be back to your best in no time.'

But sadly, it wasn't that straightforward. When Pierre-Emerick returned to training at Rouen, he was no longer 'the quick guy', the one out-sprinting everyone. He was just average now. Opposition defenders weren't going to shout, 'Watch out for the not-that-quick guy on the wing!', were they? He had lost his extra little bit of pace, and what if it never came back? It was best not to think about that possibility, but he couldn't help himself.

'I'm nothing without my superpower,' he moaned miserably. 'I may as well give up now!'

Eventually, Pierre-Emerick had no choice but to explain his feelings to his father.

'Why don't you take a short break from the game?' Yaya suggested helpfully. The last thing he wanted to do was force his son to follow in his footsteps. He just wanted him to be happy, in whatever career he chose. 'Then you can see whether you miss playing for a football team.'

Pierre-Emerick nodded glumly. It felt like he'd failed and let his dad down, but maybe he did need a fresh start...

In the end, Pierre-Emerick's break from football didn't last long, however. Life was so dull without his favourite sport! Now that he had finished school, what was he supposed to do all day? Get a job in an office or a shop? No, he had to think positively about his future.

'Well, I may as well keep myself fit,' Pierre-Emerick decided, 'even if my football career *is* over.'

So, he pushed himself hard, running sprints in the local park. Slowly but surely, his extra little bit of pace returned. What a relief! It was like having his best friend back.

'I've really missed you!' Pierre-Emerick joked to himself, while panting at the finish line.

He had really missed playing football too. He missed everything about it, but especially the excitement of scoring goals, and the pleasure of being part of a team. Pierre-Emerick wasn't ready to quit just yet – not when he had his superpower back, and not while his dream of becoming a professional was still alive. Soon enough, he had a ball back at his feet again.

'Well, I may as well keep up my skills work,' Pierre-Emerick decided, 'even if my football career *is* over.'

Fortunately for him, it wasn't. After six months of training alone, Pierre-Emerick got a phone call from his dad.

'Son, are you ready to train with a team again?'

'Yes!' Pierre-Emerick didn't even stop to think, or ask which team Yaya was talking about. He was just so desperate to get back into the game.

The team turned out to be Bastia, the biggest football club on the French island of Corsica – nearly

800 miles away from Rouen. Pierre-Emerick was on the move again, but this time, he didn't care.

'As long as I get to play, I'll be happy!'

In no time at all, Pierre-Emerick's superstar football career was back on track.

CHAPTER 8

AC MILAN PART 1: STAR IN THE MAKING

In 2007, two years after the move to Bastia, Pierre-Emerick was on the move again, and this time, it was particularly exciting news. He was off to AC Milan.

When his dad got a new job as a scout for the Italian giants, he had made his youngest son a promise:

'If you score lots of goals at Bastia, then I'll try to get you a trial at AC Milan.'

DEAL! Pierre-Emerick was already on his way to becoming Bastia's next goal machine, but now that he had his extra Italian incentive, suddenly he couldn't stop scoring.

*Goooooooooooooooooooaaaaaaaaaaaaaaaallllllllllll
lllllllllllllll!!!!!!!!!!!!!!!!!!*

*Goooooooooooooooooooaaaaaaaaaaaaaaaallllllllllll
lllllllllllllll!!!!!!!!!!!!!!!!!!*

*Goooooooooooooooooooaaaaaaaaaaaaaaaallllllllllll
lllllllllllllll!!!!!!!!!!!!!!!!!!*

'Okay, okay – I'll see what I can do!' Yaya agreed happily.

When Pierre-Emerick arrived at the AC Milan training ground for his trial, he could barely believe his eyes. It was like a football fantasy land! There were perfect grass pitches everywhere, and the equipment and facilities were all top of the range.

'I'm not going back to Bastia,' Pierre-Emerick told himself confidently. 'I'm here to stay!'

Fortunately, the AC Milan youth coaches agreed. What they saw was a raw football talent with one very special asset: super-speed.

'If he works hard on the rest of his game, that kid could be incredible!'

It was clear to see that Pierre-Emerick was a seventeen-year-old player with plenty of potential. If they gave him the right support, the club could have a superstar on their hands.

'Welcome to AC Milan!'

Pierre-Emerick was delighted. He would be staying there in Italy with his dad and his half-brothers, Catilina and Willy, who were both in the academy too.

'Imagine the three of us playing in the first team together.'

That was the family dream: Willy in defence, Catilina on the left-wing, and Pierre-Emerick up front. Perfect!

They had a long way to go before that, though. Very few youngsters were good enough to break into the AC Milan first team. Instead, it was packed with expensive signings from all over the world:

Alessandro Nesta, Andrea Pirlo and Filippo Inzaghi from other clubs in Italy,

Clarence Seedorf from the Netherlands,

Yoann Gourcuff from France,

Kakha Kaladze from Georgia,

and lots of Brazilians: Dida, Cafu, Serginho,

Emerson, Kaká, Pato, and best of all, Pierre-Emerick's ultimate football hero, Ronaldo!

Boy, it was going to be really tough, but Pierre-Emerick would do his best to make it in Milan.

His first big opportunity came in the Champions Youth Cup in Malaysia. The AC Under-19s would be up against many of the best clubs in the world: Barcelona, Juventus, Manchester United, Chelsea, Bayern Munich, Porto, Boca Juniors… The list went on and on.

Milan were in Group A with Arsenal, Ajax, and Flamengo from Brazil. All of the top football scouts would be there at the tournament, so it was the perfect stage for Pierre-Emerick to shine.

At half-time in their first match against Flamengo, AC Milan were losing 1–0. But early in the second half, their super-speedy striker saved the day. Pierre-Emerick started the move with a beautiful long ball from inside his own half. He didn't stop to admire his pass, though; no, he sprinted forward to join the attack. *ZOOM!* Oh yes, he definitely had his pace back. A Flamengo defender tried to keep up with

him, but he soon gave up. In a flash, Pierre-Emerick
was in the penalty area, controlling the return pass.
The keeper saved his first shot, but he slid in to score
the rebound.

Goooooooooooooooooooaaaaaaaaaaaaaaaaalllllllllllll
!!!

It was *1–1!* Pierre-Emerick jogged joyfully towards
the corner-flag, ready to show off his big celebration.
Unlike his style hero Sánchez, he didn't throw his
hands down to the floor; he was good enough to do
a flip from a standing start, and it looked way cooler
that way. As he landed on his feet, Pierre-Emerick
saluted the fans and then performed a quick dance
with his teammate, Kingsley Umunegbu. What an
entertainer!

And that was just the start of The Aubameyang
Show. In AC's second group match against Ajax,
Pierre-Emerick burst onto Kingsley's clever through-
ball and calmly dribbled around the keeper.

Goooooooooooooooooooaaaaaaaaaaaaaaaaalllllllllllll
!!!

This time, he celebrated with some dance moves

instead of the somersault. He was having the time of his life. Each goal gave Pierre-Emerick even more confidence to express himself. What next? Against Arsenal, he stretched out his long left leg and volleyed the ball over the keeper's head. It was a beauty, his best yet.

Goooooooooooooooooooooaaaaaaaaaaaaaaaalllllllllllll lllllllllllllll!!!!!!!!!!!!!!!!!!!!

'Man, you're on fire!' Kingsley cheered.

It was true; Pierre-Emerick was absolutely unstoppable. In the quarter-final against Bayern Munich, he opened the scoring with a really Ronaldo-esque finish. He curled the ball around the keeper and just past the sliding defender on the goal line. *1–0!*

Pierre-Emerick blew kisses to the crowd and then performed his trademark flip. He loved being football's stylish new superstar. Then in the second half, he raced through and beat the keeper to the ball.

'That's a goal, right?' Pierre-Emerick checked with the referee. The Bayern defenders were claiming that he must have been offside, but he was just too quick for them.

Yes, it was game over. *Aubameyang 2 – Bayern 0!*

Eventually, AC Milan lost to Juventus in the semi-finals, but their star striker still finished as the tournament's top scorer with seven goals.

What an incredible two weeks! Pierre-Emerick was full of belief as he returned to Italy. After years of moves and frustrations, it now felt like the future was his. Surely, with all those goals at the Champions Youth Cup, he had taken a giant step towards the AC Milan first team?

CHAPTER 9

AC MILAN PART 2: THE BOY WITH SQUARE FEET

Unfortunately, the next step wasn't so straightforward. Despite Pierre-Emerick's star performances at the Champions Youth Cup, the AC Milan youth coaches still weren't entirely convinced about his potential.

'He's quick, of course, but we have a whole bunch of players with much better technique.'

'Yeah, that boy has square feet – his touch is all over the place sometimes!'

'He might be shining in the Under-19s, but he's not going to challenge the likes of Ronaldo and Inzaghi, is he?'

Well if Pierre-Emerick couldn't persuade his own

youth coaches, what chance did he have of persuading the AC Milan first team manager, Carlo Ancelotti?

The youth coaches seemed to prefer the Italian players, who had been at the club for a long time and weren't so flashy. Pierre-Emerick, meanwhile, was often left on the bench, and used as a super sub. It was like they didn't trust him to play the whole ninety minutes.

'Hey, I'm better than that!' Pierre-Emerick sometimes felt like shouting, but he didn't. Instead, he just kept working hard in training because, although he wasn't a regular starter for the AC Milan youth team, he was learning lots. Teams in Italy were always very well-organised, with a clear shape and structure on the field.

It was Pierre-Emerick's first experience of complex football tactics, and with every tough training session, he could feel himself becoming a better player. He was understanding more and more about the game.

In the past, Pierre-Emerick would have just ran with the ball and gone for goal, but now he was thinking all the time:

What run should he make and when?

Where would his teammates want him to be?

Which would be the best option in each different situation – pass, or dribble, or shoot?

It was all great practice for the day when he would take on the defenders of Serie A, who were famous for being the best in the world.

Sadly, that day never arrived, but Pierre-Emerick did get the chance to at least train with the AC Milan first team. Nervously, he walked out onto the field to join a squad full of his football heroes – the captain Paolo Maldini, Cafu, Seedorf, Kaká, and, of course, Ronaldo. What an experience! Pierre-Emerick tried his best to act like a professional around them, but part of him just wanted to ask for photos like he was still a young fan.

'Come on, concentrate!' he told himself. He had a manager to impress.

And Ancelotti was certainly impressed. He could see straight away that Pierre-Emerick was a very dangerous young forward, with a breathtaking burst of speed. In years to come, he could become a superstar.

But at that moment, in 2008, AC Milan were fighting for all the major trophies: the Serie A title, the

Italian Cup, and best of all, the Champions League which they had won in 2007, and which they wanted to win again. And in order to do that, Ancelotti already had an amazing group of attackers to choose from:

Kaká, Pato, Inzaghi, Ronaldo, Alberto Gilardino, Alberto Paloschi...

There just wasn't room for another striker at AC Milan. Pierre-Emerick was given a shirt number – 41 – but no game-time.

At first, he waited patiently in case he got a chance to play. After all, he was learning so much from watching all the world-class players in training. But as the months flew by, he eventually decided that enough was enough. He was nineteen years old now and desperate to kick off his senior playing career. He was raring to go, and he didn't want to waste another moment.

'All I want is regular first-team football,' Pierre-Emerick told his dad. 'I don't care where!'

AC Milan agreed and so in June 2008, a loan deal was done. Pierre-Emerick would be spending the 2008–09 season at French club, Dijon.

CHAPTER 10

HAPPY DAYS AT DIJON

It felt good to be back home in France. Pierre-Emerick was excited about the loan season ahead. The Dijon manager, Faruk Hadžibegić, knew his dad well from their playing days together at Toulouse. He warmly welcomed his new signing of Pierre-Emerick and even made him the club's new Number 9.

'Wow, thanks!' Pierre-Emerick grinned, looking down at the red shirt in his hands. In his head, he was already thinking, 'Great, that means I should be getting plenty of game-time here!'

Dijon would be playing in Ligue 2, the same division as his old club, Bastia. It felt like the perfect level for Pierre-Emerick to take his first kicks as a professional footballer. The main aim for Dijon was to avoid relegation. The year before, the club had only secured their place in Ligue 2 on the very last day of the season. Could they make things a little easier for themselves this time around?

Pierre-Emerick hoped so as he arrived for his first training session.

'*Bonjour!*' most of his new teammates greeted him. One player, however, said something a little different.

'*Buongiorno!*'

Pierre-Emerick was shocked – did Dijon have an Italian in their squad? No, they didn't, but their Uruguayan forward, Sebastián Ribas, had spent two seasons at Inter Milan, AC's big local rivals. So would the two players be enemies? No, instead, they became best friends straight away.

Pierre-Emerick and Sebastián were both young and new to the club, and they bonded by sharing stories of their struggles in Italy.

'This is a fresh start, though,' they agreed happily.

MATT AND TOM OLDFIELD

'Together, we're going to light up Ligue 2!'

Pierre-Emerick escaped between the Tours centre-backs, beating the offside trap with ease. The keeper blocked his first shot, but he tapped in the rebound. *1–0!*

Gooooooooooooooooooooaaaaaaaaaaaaaaaalllllllllllll llllllllllllll!!!!!!!!!!!!!!!!!!!!

Finally, in his fourth match for Dijon, Pierre-Emerick was off the mark – and he celebrated, naturally, with a flip.

'Bravo!' Sebastián cheered as he chased after his strike partner.

With ten minutes to go, the Uruguayan won the match for Dijon with a brilliant header. *2–1!*

As Sebastián slid across the grass on his knees, Pierre-Emerick was right behind him.

'Bravo!' he cheered right back.

With the combination of Pierre-Emerick's pace and Sebastián's skill, Dijon didn't have to worry about relegation for long. The club was soon comfortably mid-table and the only way was up. It was like their two young stars had been playing

together forever. On the pitch, they often spoke
to each other in Italian so that the French defenders
didn't know what they were planning. And off the
pitch, they had lots of fun making up new dances for
all their goal celebrations.

'Yes, the fans are going to love that!'

In the last minute against Montpellier, the score
was still 0–0. Somehow. Dijon had created lots of
chances and Sebastián had even hit the crossbar.
Was there still time for a winner?

Yes! As the corner came in, Pierre-Emerick waited
near the penalty spot in lots of space. If only one of
his teammates could win the header and flick it on…
there it was, the flick he was looking for. In a flash,
Pierre-Emerick chested the ball down and smashed
a shot through the crowded box and into the roof of
the net. *1–0!*

*Gooooooooooooooooooooaaaaaaaaaaaaaaaalllllllllllll
lllllllllllllll!!!!!!!!!!!!!!!!!!!*

Pierre-Emerick was the Dijon hero. He sprinted
over to the supporters with a hand to his ear as if to
say, 'Come on, make more noise!' He performed his

flashy flip just in time, before he was mobbed by his delighted teammates.

Auba, you're a genius!

What a strike!

At the final whistle, Pierre-Emerick punched the air as the crowd let out an almighty roar. Soon, they were chanting his name – what a feeling! His childhood dream had come true. He had the fame *and* he had the glory; those were the two main reasons why he had always wanted to become a professional footballer.

Pierre-Emerick's loan spell at Dijon was working out so well. Playing week in week out, he was improving all the time. Finally, he was able to put everything he had learnt from the AC Milan superstars into action.

'Well done, kid,' Hadžibegić said, patting his young player on the back. At nineteen, Pierre-Emerick really was a superstar in the making. 'Now, get some rest – we don't want to tire you out too quickly!'

Away at Reims, Pierre-Emerick came off the bench

to inspire Dijon to victory. With four defenders chasing him, he looked up and cleverly crossed the ball to Éric Carrière. *3–1!*

'Thanks, Auba!' his teammate shouted, pointing and running over to him.

And there was still time for Pierre-Emerick to do what he did best. From wide on the left wing, he cut inside and curled a perfect shot into the top corner. *4–1!*

Gooooooooooooooooooooaaaaaaaaaaaaaaaaallllllllllll llllllllllllll!!!!!!!!!!!!!!!!!!!

Pierre-Emerick stood there saluting the Dijon supporters with a big smile on his face. What an entertainer! That was his third goal in his last six games. He was on fire again, just like at the 2007 Champions Youth Cup. Were AC Milan watching? Pierre-Emerick hoped so, but to make sure, all he could do was keep on scoring.

Against Nîmes, Sebastián flicked a header on, knowing that his strike partner was ready to pounce. *GOAL!*

Pierre-Emerick stole the ball off the Ajaccio centre-back and sent the keeper the wrong way. *GOAL!*

Pierre-Emerick made sure to show his old club Bastia what they were missing. *GOAL!*

And he was way too quick for the Vannes defence too. *GOAL!*

Dijon finished in eighth place in Ligue 2 and Pierre-Emerick finished with eight goals. Not bad at all for a nineteen-year-old playing his first full season of professional football. It was a strong start, but he knew that he still had a long way to go if he was going to prove his Milan youth coaches wrong.

'Please don't go back to Italy,' Sebastián begged. 'If you stay here, we'll win the Ligue 2 title next year for sure!'

Pierre-Emerick liked the sound of that, but for now, his loan spell in France was over. With a heavy heart, he waved goodbye to Sebastián and Dijon, and travelled back to AC Milan to find out what would happen next.

CHAPTER 11

INTERNATIONAL INTEREST

The AC Milan coaches weren't the only ones watching Pierre-Emerick during his successful debut season at Dijon. The Italy Under-19s were paying attention too and they really liked what they saw.

'How would you like to come and play for us?' their manager asked.

The call-up really surprised Pierre-Emerick. Italy? He hadn't even thought about playing for them! He had been too busy trying to make up his mind between the other three countries in his life:

France – his birthplace and his home for most of his young life.

Spain – the nation of his mum, his grandparents and his beloved Real Madrid.

Gabon – his dad's homeland and the country that he had proudly captained.

It was already a very difficult decision and Pierre-Emerick really didn't need a fourth option.

'Thank you very much for the offer, but I just don't feel Italian,' he told the Under-19s manager.

So, what *did* Pierre-Emerick feel? He certainly felt French after his childhood at Laval and his loan spell at Dijon. But thanks to all of Yaya's stories, he also felt Gabonese. Pierre-Emerick had always planned to follow in his father's footsteps, but what if he wanted to win the World Cup? France were much more likely to do that...

Fortunately, Pierre-Emerick still had some time to make up his mind. If he played for France at youth level, he could always change his mind later. And that's exactly what he did.

In February 2009, Pierre-Emerick was a second-half substitute for the France Under-21s in a friendly match against Tunisia. Instead of Number 9, he was

Number 19, but that didn't matter at all. Wearing
the famous blue shirt was something that he had
dreamed about since the 1998 World Cup, when
he was only nine years old. This was his chance to
become 'the new Thierry Henry'.

Ten minutes after Pierre-Emerick came on, Gabriel
Obertan delivered a teasing cross from the left wing.
Pierre-Emerick got in front of his marker and jumped
up high to meet it, but it flew just over his head. His
strike partner, David N'Gog, slid in at the back post
to score instead. *1–1!*

'Come on!' Pierre-Emerick cheered, grabbing the
ball out of the net.

He tried his hardest to score a winning goal, but
sadly the game ended in a disappointing draw. And
that turned out to be Pierre-Emerick's one and only
game for France.

A month later, the Gabon manager Alain Giresse
invited Pierre-Emerick to play for their senior
national team. He couldn't say no to that – if he had,
Yaya would have been furious!

Pierre-Emerick was determined to make his dad

proud and carry on his great work. Yaya had helped lead Gabon to the Africa Cup of Nations in 1994 and 1996, but The Panthers had only managed to qualify once more since then. What they needed was a new national hero who could shoot them to the 2010 tournament.

'That's going to be ME!' Pierre-Emerick declared confidently.

Together with his brother Willy, he set off on the long journey to Morocco to make his big international debut. They were Panthers now and proud to wear the yellow shirt.

'Welcome to the team!' the Gabon squad greeted them warmly. Pierre-Emerick already knew some of his new teammates because they played their club football in France. The goalkeeper Didier Ovono was at Le Mans, centre-back Bruno Ecuele Manga was at Angers, and midfielder Hervé Batoménila played with him at Dijon.

'Trust me, this guy's good,' Hervé told the others, '*REALLY* good!'

Pierre-Emerick couldn't wait to show them.

Giresse started him on the right wing and he fought hard for every ball. It was hard to believe that Pierre-Emerick was playing international football already, before he had even played for AC Milan, but he was fully focused on his task. Although Morocco were one of the best teams in Africa, if he could just get one chance to show off his super-speed...

As soon as the ball was played through, *ZOOM!* he was off, sprinting after it. The Morocco defenders had made a terrible mistake; they had given him a headstart in a race that he was always going to win. On the edge of the penalty area, he slowed down and calmly picked his spot – bottom right. *1–0!*

Goooooooooooooooooooaaaaaaaaaaaaaaaalllllllllllll llllllllllllll!!!!!!!!!!!!!!!!!!!!!

A goal during his Gabon debut, and with his dad watching! Pierre-Emerick tried to act cool, but it wasn't easy in all the excitement. Yes, he had definitely made the right decision by choosing to play for Gabon. He flipped his body through the air and then pointed up at the fans as if to say, 'That one's for you!' There would be many more to come.

Just before half-time, Roguy Méyé made it 2-0.
'Yes!' Pierre-Emerick cried out, throwing his arms up
in the air. He already felt like a central part of
the team.

If they kept this up, Gabon could qualify for
the Africa Cup of Nations again, and who knew,
maybe even the 2010 FIFA World Cup. They had
to dream big.

In the end, The Panthers missed out on playing at
their first-ever World Cup, but they did book their
place at the next Africa Cup of Nations. The future
looked bright. Gabon were back in the big time,
and in Pierre-Emerick, they had found their new
national hero.

CHAPTER 12

FRUSTRATING TIMES IN FRANCE

Pierre-Emerick had passed his first French test at Dijon in Ligue 2. Next, it was time for test number two: playing on loan in Ligue 1 for Lille. The AC Milan coaches were keen to see how well their speedy young striker would cope against better defences.

'Fine, I'll show them!' Pierre-Emerick thought positively.

At first, the loan move went smoothly. The Lille manager Rudi Garcia handed Pierre-Emerick the Number 11 shirt and picked him to play against Genk in the Europa League qualifying round. Although he didn't score himself, Pierre-Emerick set up two goals for his teammates.

First, he pounced on some poor defending and back-heeled a clever pass to Eden Hazard. *3–1!*

Then, three minutes later, Pierre-Emerick controlled a long ball beautifully, dribbled into the penalty area and cut it back to Túlio de Melo. *4–1!*

'What a cross, Auba!' the Brazilian called out, hugging him.

So far so good, but once the Ligue 1 season started, things started to go wrong for Pierre-Emerick. Compared to his time at Dijon, there was a lot more competition for places at Lille. After a disappointing performance against Marseille, Garcia dropped him from the team. The manager was still searching for his best attack and when he found it, he stuck with it:

Hazard on the left,

Gervinho on the right,

Túlio in the middle,

and Pierre-Emerick on the bench.

Pierre-Emerick had hoped to get lots of game-time ahead of the Africa Cup of Nations but instead, he hardly played at all. By the time that tournament started in January 2010, Pierre-Emerick had only just scored his first goal for Lille. It was so frustrating.

'I may as well be back at Milan,' he complained to his dad. 'I'm not improving at all; in fact, I think I'm getting worse!'

What Pierre-Emerick needed was an amazing Africa Cup of Nations to lift his spirits, but instead, his goal troubles continued. Right when Gabon needed their new national hero to shine, he failed to score against Cameroon, Tunisia or Gambia. It was like he'd left his shooting boots back in Dijon with Sebastián.

'I'm sorry, I've let you all down,' Pierre-Emerick told his Gabon teammates in the dressing room. After only one win in three games, their tournament was over, and it felt like it was all his fault.

'Hey, don't worry, we'll be back!' Bruno Ecuele Manga reassured him.

In the meantime, Pierre-Emerick returned to Lille and his life on the bench. Even when he eventually came on and scored the winning goal against Stade

Rennais, it didn't make a difference. For the next match, he was still a sub.

'What am I doing?' Pierre-Emerick asked himself angrily. 'I'm nearly twenty-one now – I need to be playing every week!'

He couldn't wait for his loan at Lille to end so that he could try again somewhere else. Surely, things couldn't get any worse than two goals in fourteen games? Actually, they could, and they did.

For the 2010–11 season, AC Milan decided to send Pierre-Emerick back to France to take his Ligue 1 test for the second time.

'You'll like Monaco a lot more, though,' Yaya promised him. 'It's very flashy, just like you!'

Pierre-Emerick really hoped that his dad was right. He needed this loan move to go well – as well as Dijon, if not better. Otherwise, where would he have to go next – Ligue 2 again? No way!

Monaco was a big, famous football club, where one of Pierre-Emerick's heroes, George Weah, had won lots of trophies in the 1990s. They weren't doing so well anymore, but he was there to help turn things around. That was the plan, anyway.

Just like at Lille, Pierre-Emerick got off to a good start. In his third match away at Lens, he scored one of his best goals ever. The long throw-in looked like it was going way over his head, but in a flash, he swivelled his body around and somehow lifted his leg high enough to volley the ball in off the crossbar. *2–0!*

Goooooooooooooooooooooaaaaaaaaaaaaaaaaallllllllllllll lllllllllllllll!!!!!!!!!!!!!!!!!!!!

What a strike! In his delight, Pierre-Emerick pounded the Monaco badge on his shirt again and again. He wanted the whole world to know:

'I'm back!'

He scored another goal against Auxerre and then dribbled all the way from the edge of his own penalty area to set one up for Ju-yeong Park against Marseille.

'Excellent work!' praised his manager Guy Lacombe.

After that, however, it quickly fell apart. He wasn't scoring goals anymore, and his team wasn't winning anymore. They lost so many matches that they slipped all the way down into the Ligue 1 relegation zone.

'This is a disaster!' Pierre-Emerick muttered as Monaco slumped to yet another defeat.

By January 2011, Lacombe was gone and so was Pierre-Emerick, after scoring just two goals in nineteen games. The new Monaco manager, Laurent Banide, decided that he didn't need a flashy young forward and sent him back to Italy.

Pierre-Emerick was going to have to return to AC Milan six months earlier than expected. How humiliating! But fortunately, another French club agreed to take a chance on him. Saint-Étienne were in a much better position than Monaco. In fact, their manager, Christophe Galtier, was aiming to qualify for the Europa League.

'But we need more speed,' he explained to Pierre-Emerick, 'and more goals too.'

'Cool, I can certainly help with that!' he grinned.

Pierre-Emerick had a good feeling about his latest move. Saint-Étienne did have quite a few strikers already, but he was going to work extra hard to earn his chance to play.

'You'll see,' he told Galtier with a focused look on his face.

Pierre-Emerick started off on the bench, but he didn't stay there for long. The Saint-Étienne manager could see how determined he was, and the team was really struggling to score.

'Go out there and prove yourself!' Galtier urged him on.

'Thanks, Coach!'

Pierre-Emerick could feel his form improving again, but unfortunately, the goals still weren't flowing. By the end of the season, he had only scored two goals in fourteen games – the same numbers he had got during his loan at Lille. That was nowhere near good enough for a top-class forward.

What next for Pierre-Emerick? That summer of 2011 felt like a massive crossroads moment in his football career. If he wasn't careful, he would end up playing in the lower leagues of France forever.

He really didn't want that, but what could he do to raise his game?

'If you keep working hard,' his dad told him, 'it will all work out in the end.'

Really? Pierre-Emerick didn't want to just sit back and wait. What he needed was a coach who believed in him. But most of all, he needed to believe in himself.

CHAPTER 13

SCORING AGAIN AT SAINT-ÉTIENNE

For Pierre-Emerick, it was his like his youth days all over again – always on the move. He was desperate to settle down and stay at one club for at least one whole season, and he wanted that club to be Saint-Étienne. Their quick, counter-attacking style of play suited him perfectly. Plus, he liked the manager, and Galtier liked him back. However, Pierre-Emerick knew that he still needed to prove himself as a natural goalscorer.

'The most important thing is hitting the target,' his manager had told him at his first Saint-Étienne training session. 'You could strike the most powerful shot in the world, but if it doesn't land between the posts, it's not going to be a goal, is it? If it's on target, though, even if it's straight at the keeper, you never know what might happen – a bad bounce, a silly slip… You've got to at least make the goalie make the save.'

Those words stayed with Pierre-Emerick that summer, as he prepared for the biggest season of his career. It was time for him to get serious about scoring. Soon, his first son would be born, and he would need to provide for him. His goals would have to pay the bills. Plus, of course, Pierre-Emerick wanted Aubameyang Jr to be proud of his dad's performances.

So, he practised and practised, shooting from lots of different distances and from every possible angle. Pierre-Emerick worked like crazy, all summer long, until at last he could feel his confidence coming back.

'Just give me one more season,' he told Galtier. 'You won't regret it!'

When Pierre-Emerick returned to Saint-Étienne for preseason, he was like a completely different player.

The manager could see a new fire in his eyes, and a new accuracy in his finishing.

Goooooooooooooooooooaaaaaaaaaaaaaaaaalllllllllllll lllllllllllllll!!!!!!!!!!!!!!!!!!!!!!

Goooooooooooooooooooaaaaaaaaaaaaaaaaalllllllllllll lllllllllllllll!!!!!!!!!!!!!!!!!!!!!!

Goooooooooooooooooooaaaaaaaaaaaaaaaaalllllllllllll lllllllllllllll!!!!!!!!!!!!!!!!!!!!!!

The old Auba was back with a *BANG!* A big grin spread across Galtier's face. If Pierre-Emerick could combine his super-speed with super-shooting, that was a recipe for real success. Even though Saint-Étienne had sold some of their best players during the summer, they had found themselves a new star striker.

Pierre-Emerick couldn't wait for the 2011–12 season to start. Saint-Étienne's first game was a tough trip to Bordeaux, but the team's new strikeforce made it look easy.

Bakary Sako escaped down the left wing and delivered a cross so dangerous that the Bordeaux defender could only kick it into his own net. *1–0!*

'Great work, that's your goal really!' Pierre-Emerick cheered, high-fiving Bakary.

Now, it was his turn to score a second goal and secure the three points for Saint-Étienne. In the thirtieth minute, a Bordeaux defender cleared the ball straight to Pierre-Emerick. He was out wide on the right wing, but what was it Galtier had told him? 'The most important thing is hitting the target'…

BANG! Pierre-Emerick struck the ball sweetly and it sailed high over the keeper's head. But to everyone's surprise, it struck the post and went in. *2–0!*

Goooooooooooooooooooaaaaaaaaaaaaaaaallllllllllllll lllllllllllll!!!!!!!!!!!!!!!!!!!!

Was it meant to be a cross or a shot? Who cared? It was a goal! Pierre-Emerick certainly didn't care as he flipped his body through the air and then danced joyfully with Bakary and Josuha Guilavogui.

One game, one goal – Pierre-Emerick was off to another strong start. The big question now was: could he keep the goals flowing this time?

Yes! He scored against Sochaux and Stade Rennais

and Évian. Then on a rainy night against Stade
Brestois 29, Pierre-Emerick grabbed two more goals.

In the first half, he ran in at the back post to tap in
Max Gradel's cross. *1–0!*

And in the second half, Albin Ebondo played a ball
down the right wing for Pierre-Emerick to chase.
ZOOM! He got there first, of course, and then calmly
slotted his shot between the keeper's legs. *Nutmeg!*

*Goooooooooooooooooooooaaaaaaaaaaaaaaaaallllllllllllll
lllllllllllllll!!!!!!!!!!!!!!!!!!!!*

Pierre-Emerick was delighted to be scoring so
many goals. His baby son Curtys would be very
proud of his successful dad. All that hard work over
the summer was really paying off, but he couldn't
relax now. No, he had to keep improving.

'What could I do better?' Pierre-Emerick always
asked himself, and asked all the Saint-Étienne
coaches too. That's what being a professional
footballer was all about.

Whenever he missed a good chance in a match, he
would practise that move over and over again until
he got it right. And Pierre-Emerick didn't just want to

be a better striker; he wanted to be a better all-round player. As well as scoring more, he was also creating more chances for his teammates. In Saint-Étienne's 2–0 win over Caen, he helped set up both goals for Bănel Nicoliţă and then Bakary.

'Thanks, Auba!'

Saint-Étienne had the option to sign him permanently at the end of the season, but their manager didn't want to wait until then, and neither did Pierre-Emerick. Galtier wanted to get the deal done before other top European clubs came along and offered AC Milan more money. So, in December 2011, Saint-Étienne paid £1.6 million to buy Pierre-Emerick. What a bargain!

'I am really pleased to sign permanently,' he told the media. 'This is one of the best spells of my career, and I can't wait for it to continue.'

Pierre-Emerick was at Saint-Étienne to stay. He celebrated in style out on the football pitch against Lorient.

Early in the second half, Laurent Batlles slipped a beautiful pass through to Pierre-Emerick. As the keeper rushed out towards him, he pretended that he was going to hit a really powerful shot into the top left corner. But once the keeper started his dive, Pierre-Emerick slid the ball into the opposite side of the net instead. *1–0!*

Goooooooooooooooooooooaaaaaaaaaaaaaaaaalllllllllllll llllllllllllll!!!!!!!!!!!!!!!!!!!

'What a classy finish, mate!' Bakary cheered as they danced together near the corner flag.

Ten minutes later, he crossed the ball into the box, knowing exactly where his friend would be. *2–1!*

Goooooooooooooooooooooaaaaaaaaaaaaaaaaalllllllllllll llllllllllllll!!!!!!!!!!!!!!!!!!!

'Thanks, you're the best!' Pierre-Emerick shouted as he gave Bakary a big hug.

Pierre-Emerick had scored two goals in a single game for Saint-Étienne before, but never three. Would he get one last chance? In the final minute of the match, Pierre-Emerick raced through the middle to collect Lynel Kitambala's long pass. This was his chance, and he wasn't going to miss it. He calmly chested the ball down and shot past the keeper.

Goooooooooooooooooooaaaaaaaaaaaaaaaalllllllllll llllllllllllll!!!!!!!!!!!!!!!!!!!!

Not only had Pierre-Emerick scored a hat-trick, but he had scored a perfect hat-trick: one goal with his right foot, one with his left foot, and one with his head.

'Yes, Auba!' Max Gradel cried out as he jumped up on his talented teammate's back.

Pierre-Emerick's perfect hat-trick took him up to eleven goals for the season, and pushed Saint-Étienne up to fourth place in Ligue 1. If they could stay there, they would be playing Europa League football next year!

'Come on, we can do this!' Galtier encouraged his players.

But despite more goals from Pierre-Emerick, Saint-Étienne finished the season in seventh place. There would be no European adventure this time, but why not next year? Now that Pierre-Emerick had got serious about scoring goals, there was no stopping him.

CHAPTER 14

GABON'S GOAL MACHINE

The year 2012 was a landmark year for Pierre-Emerick in football, both with his club and his country. In January, he travelled to Gabon to play in the Africa Cup of Nations. This time, they were the tournament hosts and Pierre-Emerick was determined to at least get through the group stage. The previous tournament, in 2010, had been the warm-up, the wake-up call; this now was the real thing.

The Panthers had a new manager, Gernot Rohr, but their squad was still pretty much the same. Well, except Pierre-Emerick, who was now a completely different player.

'Trust me, this is going to be *MY* tournament,' he told his teammates confidently.

At club level, Pierre-Emerick was playing the best football of his life. Saint-Étienne's Goal Machine was about to become Gabon's Goal Machine.

In their first match, Stéphane N'Guéma dribbled down the right wing and floated a cross towards the back post. The Niger keeper jumped and stretched his arms up high, but he couldn't reach it. Pierre-Emerick, however, could. *1–0!*

That goal really got the party started. The home crowd went wild as Pierre-Emerick hurdled the advertising boards so that he could celebrate closer to the fans. He waved and blew kisses like a true entertainer.

Then, just before half-time, Pierre-Emerick's diving header was saved, but Stéphane scored the rebound. *2–0!*

What a start, and Gabon's good form continued against Morocco. Almost three years earlier, Pierre-Emerick had scored against them on his international debut against Morocco, and now he did it again. He volleyed the ball into the back of the net from the edge of the area. *1–1!*

Goooooooooooooooooooooaaaaaaaaaaaaaaaaallllllllllll llllllllllllllll!!!!!!!!!!!!!!!!!!!!

A loud roar rang out around the stadium. The Gabon supporters hugged and danced, and so did their football heroes on the pitch.

'Yes, Auba!'

'What a beauty!'

'Come on, we can win this!'

Pierre-Emerick wasn't following in his father's footsteps anymore; he was overtaking him as the new national hero. With the crowd behind him, he set up a second goal for Daniel Cousin and Gabon won 3–2. The Panthers had done it; they were through to the Africa Cup of Nations quarter-finals for the first time since 1996, since the glory days of Pierre-Emerick's dad.

'Well done, son!' Yaya cheered as proud tears filled his eyes.

There was still one group game to go, and Pierre-Emerick didn't want to rest. No way, he wanted to play and win and score, and that's exactly what he did. He made it three wins for Gabon, and three goals for Auba. Pierre-Emerick had been right all along; it really was *his* tournament.

Or at least, it was his tournament *so far*. He couldn't get carried away. Gabon were still two games away from the Africa Cup of Nations Final, and next up was Mali. The two teams were very evenly-matched and he would need to be at his very best.

Pierre-Emerick did set up Gabon's only goal of the game, but he also missed some glorious scoring chances of his own. Oh well, at least they were winning. But not for long – Mali scored a late equaliser and, in the end, the quarter-final went all the way to penalties.

When Pierre-Emerick walked forward to take his penalty, the score was 3–3. No-one had missed so far in the shoot-out and so the pressure was really on. His country was counting on him. Max usually took the penalties at Saint-Étienne, but Pierre-Emerick always practised them in training.

He hardly ever missed, but there was extra pressure here: this was the Africa Cup of Nations quarter-final.

'Stay cool,' he told himself as he placed the ball down on the spot.

On the outside, Pierre-Emerick was smiling, but on the inside, he felt more nervous than he had for years.

He ran up slowly, stuttering to see if the keeper would dive early. He didn't and he guessed the right way. *SAVED!*

Arghhhh! Pierre-Emerick couldn't believe it. What a mistake! Why had he tried to place the ball in the bottom corner, instead of striking it with power? He turned away and lifted his shirt up to cover his face. Right then, he wished he could be anywhere, anywhere except there on that football pitch, in front of thousands of sad faces.

Gabon now needed a Mali player to miss. Pierre-Emerick could hardly watch as the final penalty was taken. The keeper dived the right way, his fingertips almost grazing the ball, but it wasn't quite enough.

As the ball rolled in, Pierre-Emerick cried and cried. Their tournament – *his* tournament – was over, and it was all his fault. Although his teammates tried to comfort him, it was no use. Eventually, his dad had to help him off the field.

'It's okay, it's okay,' Yaya kept repeating. 'These things happen. You're still young, son – you'll be back!'

Pierre-Emerick still finished as the tournament's top goalscorer, but his pain lasted a long time. Fortunately, he soon had another international competition to look forward to. Back in December 2011, Gabon had won the U-23 African Championships, beating Morocco in the final. The champions received a trophy and also, best of all, a place at the 2012 Olympic Games. Gabon had never qualified before, and at the age of twenty-three, Pierre-Emerick was still young enough to play.

'London, here we come!' he celebrated with Bruno. They would get to play at Wembley, one of the most famous football stadiums in the world.

Plus, this was a golden chance for Pierre-Emerick

to make up for his mistake at the Africa Cup of Nations. Gabon were in a group with Switzerland, Mexico and South Korea. It wouldn't be easy, but he was going to do his best to become a national hero again.

The Panthers, however, got off to the worst possible start. In only the fourth minute, Switzerland's Innocent Emeghara beat Henri Ndong to the ball in the box. *Foul. Penalty. 1–0!*

Pierre-Emerick wasn't giving up, though. Gabon still had more than eighty-five minutes to grab an equaliser...

In the last minute of the first half, Alexander N'Doumbou dribbled forward down the left wing. As he looked up for the cross, Pierre-Emerick made his move between the Switzerland centre-backs. The pass was perfect, and so was the first touch and the finish through the keeper's legs. *1–1!*

Goooooooooooooooooooooaaaaaaaaaaaaaaaallllllllllll llllllllllllll!!!!!!!!!!!!!!!!!!!

Pierre-Emerick was the first Gabonese player ever to score at the Olympics! He celebrated with a trademark flip and then stood by the corner flag with his arms out wide, waiting for his teammates to join him. Surely, all was forgiven now?

'We love you, Auba!'

Gabon held on for the draw against Switzerland, but they lost their next match to Mexico. That meant they would have to beat South Korea in their final group game to make it through to the quarter-finals.

Sadly, it wasn't to be. But Pierre-Emerick and the other Panthers returned home with their heads held high and their country's first-ever Olympic goal, scored by Gabon's greatest goal machine.

CHAPTER 15

TROPHY TIME

In his fantastic first full season at Saint-Étienne in 2011–12, Pierre-Emerick had finished with sixteen goals and eleven assists. Those were excellent figures, but could he become even better? His manager, Christophe Galtier, believed so, and most importantly, he himself believed so.

'I'm only twenty-three,' Pierre-Emerick discussed with his dad, 'and I'm still learning. Trust me, there's plenty more to come. This season, I'm going to score as many goals as Zlatan. Actually no – MORE!'

Zlatan Ibrahimović was the new star striker for Paris Saint-Germain. The club was desperate to win the Ligue 1 title, and so they had spent lots of money on big new signings. And Zlatan was the biggest of them all. At Pierre-Emerick's old club AC Milan, the Swedish hero had scored thirty-five goals in one season!

If he wanted to become a world-class striker, Pierre-Emerick had to aim for Zlatan's level. He wasn't as tall and strong as Zlatan, but he was the fastest footballer around.

'Wow!' Galtier couldn't believe the numbers on his stopwatch screen. 'Auba, you just ran the 100 metres in eleven seconds. You could be an Olympic sprinter!'

Panting at the finish line, Pierre-Emerick allowed himself a smile. Good, he was up to full speed ahead of the new season. He didn't want to be 'the new Usain Bolt', however. No, he wanted to be 'the new Thierry Henry' or 'the new Ronaldo'.

Pierre-Emerick's friend, Bakary Sako, had moved to English club Wolves, but Max Gradel was still there, and Saint-Étienne had signed a new winger called Romain Hamouma. Romain understood the team's game-plan straight away – attack as quickly as possible.

Romain raced down the right wing and crossed it to Pierre-Emerick in the middle. *1–0!*

Pierre-Emerick sprinted from the halfway line all the way into the penalty area. His shot hit the post, but Romain grabbed the rebound. *2–0!*

As Fabien Lemoine chipped a pass over the top, Pierre-Emerick timed his run perfectly. As the ball bounced down on the edge of the box, he took the shot early. *4–0!*

'Auba, you're amazing!' Max cheered as he jumped on his back.

After ten league games, Pierre-Emerick had scored six goals, while Zlatan had scored ten. It was time for France's two star strikers to go head to head. As the match kicked off at the Parc Des Princes, however, only one of them was out there on the pitch. And it wasn't Pierre-Emerick.

'Why am I sat on the bench?' he moaned to his fellow sub, Alejandro Alonso. 'This is our biggest game of the season!'

As the minutes ticked by, Pierre-Emerick grew more and more frustrated.

'I should be out there scoring,' he muttered to himself. 'The manager's making a big mistake!'

By half-time, he was raring to go, just as Galtier had hoped, and finally, with fifty-two minutes played, Pierre-Emerick entered the field with a point to prove. And three minutes later, Saint-Étienne were winning.

As Fabien dribbled forward from midfield, *ZOOM!* Pierre-Emerick was off, sprinting down the left wing. 'Now!' he called out as he burst into the box. He raced past Thiago Silva and then looked for Brandão in the middle. The cross didn't reach the Brazilian, though, because a PSG defender deflected it into his own net. *1–0!*

Pierre-Emerick jogged towards the corner flag with his arms out wide as if to say, 'See, that's what I can do!'

But what would Zlatan do at the other end? Fifteen minutes later, he stormed into a tackle against the Saint-Étienne keeper with his right leg raised dangerously high. He caught Stéphane Ruffier in the chest, and the referee pulled out a red card.

Not only were PSG losing 1–0, but now, they had lost their star striker too. It was time for Pierre-Emerick to win it for his team.

Alejandro came off the bench and won the ball just inside his own half. On the counter-attack, Saint-Étienne had a two-on-one situation – Alejandro and Pierre-Emerick versus Thiago Silva. As he approached the penalty area, Alejandro slid the ball across to Pierre-Emerick, who slid it under the PSG keeper. *2–0!*

Goooooooooooooooooooooaaaaaaaaaaaaaaaallllllllllll lllllllllllllll!!!!!!!!!!!!!!!!!!!

Together, the two super subs had won the game for Saint-Étienne. They celebrated with the fans by the corner flag.

'What a pass!'

'What a finish!'

Although Pierre-Emerick beat Zlatan that day, over the whole season, the Swedish star was victorious. He grabbed thirty goals as PSG won the league. They finished twelve points ahead of runners-up Marseille and twenty points ahead of Saint-Étienne in fifth place.

Pierre-Emerick did come second in the scoring charts, though. With nineteen goals and thirteen assists, he had successfully become an even better striker.

Plus, he was also challenging Zlatan as Ligue 1's flashiest superstar. During the warm-up for a match against Lyon, Pierre-Emerick decided to wear a very special, sparkling pair of boots.

'Woah, where did you get those?' Max teased him. 'They're hurting my eyes!'

As the 2012–13 season came to an end, Pierre-Emerick had his eyes on another flashy prize. Saint-Étienne were about to take on Rennes in the final of the French League Cup, having not won a major trophy since 1981 – surely, it was time for them to change that?

'Look, I know we finished eight places above them in the league, but that means nothing now,' Galtier told his players before kick-off. 'In a one-off game, anyone can win, so let's make sure it's us!'

Pierre-Emerick was really pumped up for his first-ever cup final. He even had a cool new haircut and some flashy new footwear for the big event. This was his chance to play football at the Stade de France, in front of almost 80,000 fans. What could be better than that?

'Winning,' he told himself. 'And hopefully, scoring too!'

When the two teams walked out onto the pitch, the atmosphere was incredible. As Pierre-Emerick looked up, the green of Saint-Étienne clashed with the red of Rennes. What a battle it was going to be. A moment of magic could make all the difference…

Pierre-Emerick back-heeled the ball down the line to Renaud Cohade and then kept running forward for the return pass. When it arrived, *ZOOM!* Pierre-Emerick was in behind the Rennes defence, with Brandão waiting in the box. Should he cross it with his weaker left foot? No – instead, he curled the ball in with the outside of his right foot. Pierre-Emerick's pass was so perfect that his teammate couldn't miss. *1–0 to Saint-Étienne!*

Brandão rushed over to celebrate with Pierre-Emerick, followed by Fabien and Renaud and Josuha…

'Auba, you're a genius!'

Pierre-Emerick was proud of his amazing assist, and he nearly got another. This time, he skipped past down the right wing and picked out Brandão at the back post. His header was on target – but the keeper saved it.

'Noooo!' the Brazilian groaned.

'Unlucky, keep going!' Pierre-Emerick encouraged him.

Would that one goal be enough? In the end, it was. When the final whistle blew, Pierre-Emerick threw his arms up above his head and hugged his Saint-Étienne teammates. They had done it; the trophy was theirs!

Eventually, the exhausted players slowly made their way up the stadium steps to collect their rewards. Each of them received a mini version of the League Cup itself. When the big moment arrived, Pierre-Emerick held his trophy up high. It would go nicely on his shelf at home, next to his Ligue 1 African Player of the Year award.

Campeones, Campeones, Olé! Olé! Olé!

CHAPTER 16

DREAM DEBUTS AT DORTMUND

Now that Pierre-Emerick was a French League Cup winner, would Saint-Étienne be able to hold on to their superstar striker? Galtier hoped so, but it wouldn't be easy. Suddenly, lots of Europe's top clubs wanted to buy Pierre-Emerick:

PSG in France,

Schalke 04 and Borussia Dortmund in Germany,

Roma and Fiorentina in Italy,

Tottenham and Newcastle United in England.

Russian club Rubin Kazan were the first to make an offer, but Saint-Étienne said no straight away. They wanted more money for their most valuable player.

By the end of June 2013, there were two teams leading the race: Newcastle and Dortmund.

Pierre-Emerick had a difficult decision to make. On the one hand, he loved the idea of playing in the Premier League, the best league in the world. With his speed, he was sure he could become a star at St James' Park, even if Newcastle weren't yet challenging for the title.

But on the other hand, playing in the Bundesliga would be exciting too, and he had heard great things about the Dortmund manager, Jürgen Klopp. He had a great reputation for developing young players, and he was offering him a chance to play in the Champions League.

In the end, it was Klopp who made his mind up for him. Just when it looked like Pierre-Emerick was about to sign for Newcastle, the Dortmund manager spoke to his dad.

'I truly believe that this is the right club for your son,' Klopp persuaded him. 'My team's style of play will suit Pierre-Emerick perfectly. We'll make the most of his speed and turn him into a world-class superstar. He'll score lots of goals and win lots of trophies here.'

Yaya was impressed, and so was Pierre-Emerick. During the previous season, Dortmund had finished second in the Bundesliga and reached the Champions League final. In both competitions, it was Bayern Munich who had beaten them. Dortmund's young forward, Mario Götze, had just moved to Bayern, which meant that Klopp needed a new attacker to play alongside Marco Reus and Robert Lewandowski.

'That's going to be me!' Pierre-Emerick said excitedly.

In early July, the deal was done, and he was officially a Dortmund player. He posed for photos with Klopp and the club's other two new signings:

A big Greek centre-back called Sokratis Papastathopoulos,

And a playmaker from Armenia called Henrikh Mkhitaryan.

'You've all got such long names!' their new manager laughed. 'I can say Sokratis, but from now on, you're Mkhi and you're Auba, okay?'

'Okay!'

After three tiring weeks of preseason training, Pierre-Emerick couldn't wait to make his competitive debut in the yellow-and-black shirt. The new season started with the Supercup: Dortmund versus Bayern Munich.

'Bring it on!' Pierre-Emerick was really looking forward to his first taste of Germany's biggest football rivalry. He was starting on the bench, but hopefully he would get a chance to shine in the second half.

With sixty minutes gone, Dortmund were 3–1 up, but then Arjen Robben pulled one back for Bayern. Uh oh, were they going to lose again? No, Dortmund just needed to hold on and hit Bayern on the counter-attack.

'Auba, get warmed up!' one of the coaches shouted.

At last! Pierre-Emerick was raring to go. All he needed was one good pass and his pace would do the rest.

As Robert collected the ball just inside the Bayern half, Pierre-Emerick was already on the run. *ZOOM!*

He was past the left-back before he had even noticed him. As two defenders closed Robert down, he played the pass that Pierre-Emerick had been hoping for.

Should he cross it to Marco or go for glory himself? Although Pierre-Emerick was desperate to score, he didn't want to seem too selfish, especially on his debut. He was into the penalty area now, so there was no time left to think. At the crucial moment, he slipped on the wet pitch, but the ball still reached its target: Marco, who guided it into the net. *4–2!*

The Yellow Wall of Dortmund fans behind the goal jumped to their feet, making as much noise as they possibly could. Pierre-Emerick had never seen, or heard, anything like it.

'You better get used to that,' Marco said with a smile as they high-fived happily. 'Great pass, by the way!'

Pierre-Emerick felt like he was part of the team already, and soon, it was a trophy-winning team. As the captain Sven Bender lifted the Super Cup above his head, the players let out a loud roar behind him.

Hurraaaaaaaaaaaaaaaaaaaaaaay!!!!

What a start to the season! After that dream Dortmund debut, Pierre-Emerick counted down the days until his first Bundesliga game.

Even though they were playing away at Augsburg, Klopp picked all three of his top forwards:

Marco on the left,

Robert in the middle,

and Pierre-Emerick on the right.

'Let's do this!' they cheered together.

Midway through the first half, Marcel Schmelzer swung the ball in from the left. It flew over Robert's head and started to drop down in front of Pierre-Emerick. He could reach it, he was sure of it, but it would require a dramatic diving header. *1–0!*

Gooooooooooooooooooooaaaaaaaaaaaaaaaallllllllllllll llllllllllllll!!!!!!!!!!!!!!!!!!!

Pierre-Emerick scrambled to his feet and looked to make sure – yes, the ball was in the net!

'Thanks, great cross!' he shouted, giving Marcel a grateful hug.

At half-time, it was still 1–0, but as Augsburg

pushed forward looking for an equaliser, Dortmund took full advantage.

Marco played the ball into Pierre-Emerick's path, knowing that he'd beat any defender in a race. He was right. After a couple of touches, Pierre-Emerick curled a shot into the bottom corner. *2–0!*

'I love playing for this team!' he cheered, throwing his arms around Marco.

Pierre-Emerick was now on a hat-trick on his Bundesliga debut. And he had thirty more minutes to get that third goal, as long as Klopp didn't take him off.

All he needed was one good pass and Pierre-Emerick's pace would do the rest. Again, it was Robert who played it, poking the ball in between the Augsburg centre-backs. Pierre-Emerick was on to it in a flash. These days, he never missed a chance like that. He dribbled around the keeper and shot into the empty net. *3–0!*

HAT-TRICK! It was hugs and smiles all round as Pierre-Emerick made his way back to the halfway line. Who said it would be hard for him to settle in at a new club in a new country? With teammates like these, football was so fun and easy!

'How does it feel to be a Dortmund hero already?' Marcel laughed, patting the club badge on Pierre-Emerick's shirt.

'Unbelievable!'

CHAPTER 17

LEARNING FROM LEWANDOWSKI

After that amazing start, the Dortmund fans had high expectations for Pierre-Emerick.

'Now that we've got Auba, Bayern don't stand a chance!'

'Yeah, he might even be better than Lewandowski!'

But Pierre-Emerick wasn't on that world-class level just yet. There was one thing that Robert had that Pierre-Emerick still needed to add to his game – consistency.

One week, he might score a hat-trick, like he did against Augsburg, but then the next, he might miss a hat-trick of chances. It was all or nothing with

Pierre-Emerick. After a few quiet games, suddenly he was on fire again versus Hamburg. He used his super-speed and super-shooting to score two goals and set one up for Robert.

Auba! Auba! Auba!

The Dortmund supporters liked the fact that he was an unpredictable player, because it made him more exciting to watch. They never knew what Auba would do next! But was that what Klopp was looking for? If Pierre-Emerick wanted to start every match, he needed to be more reliable, like Robert, who hardly ever missed the target, and who was able to score goals almost every single game.

'How do you do it?' Pierre-Emerick asked his teammate during their shooting drills in training.

Robert shrugged and smiled. 'It's all about focus and confidence. And if I do miss one, I just make sure that I score the next one.'

Pierre-Emerick laughed. 'That sounds so easy, Lewy!'

'It is, once you find your feet. But don't be too hard on yourself, Auba; it takes time to adapt to this league. Trust me, in my first year in Germany, I was nowhere near this good!'

Pierre-Emerick felt a bit better after that. His debut season at Dortmund was a big learning experience, and he was doing just fine. He was playing in one of the best leagues in the world now, and he was also playing in the Champions League.

It was a dream come true to be starring in Europe's biggest competition, even if Pierre-Emerick was mostly used as a speedy super sub for now. He helped set up Robert's winning goal against Arsenal and then scored one of his own against Napoli.

Pierre-Emerick started the counter-attack from inside the Dortmund half. He passed the ball forward to Robert and then *ZOOM!* he raced down the right wing for the one-two.

'Now, Lewy!'

The angle was tight, and the keeper was rushing out towards him, but Pierre-Emerick coolly lobbed the ball over him and into the net. *3–1!*

Goooooooooooooooooooooooaaaaaaaaaaaaaaaaaallllllllllll lllllllllllllll!!!!!!!!!!!!!!!!!!!!

114

Pierre-Emerick had just scored his first-ever Champions League goal, and the Dortmund subs ran over to celebrate with him.

'Yes, Auba – what a finish!'

Robert was next to arrive, and he wrapped his teammate in a great big hug. 'Come on!' he roared.

Thanks to Pierre-Emerick's cheeky chip, Dortmund were through to the Round of 16. And with a win over Zenit Saint Petersburg, they moved into the quarter-finals where they faced... Real Madrid!

'No way!' Pierre-Emerick felt mixed emotions when he heard the news.

On the one hand, it would be amazing to finally play at the real Bernabéu, rather than the imaginary version he had created in his bedroom as a young boy. And he would be going head-to-head with superstars like Cristiano Ronaldo and Sergio Ramos. But on the other hand, he was still a big Real Madrid fan. Was he prepared to knock out his favourite football team?

Yes! As Pierre-Emerick walked out onto the Bernabéu pitch, he was fully focused, just like Robert had told him to be. He had goals to score, and a game to win.

Unfortunately, that positivity didn't last long. In the third minute, Gareth Bale burst into the Dortmund box and poked the ball past Roman Weidenfeller. *1–0!*

Real attacked again and again, and Pierre-Emerick spent most of the time defending in his own half. He did, however, have two decent chances to score. But he blasted the first shot high over the bar and dragged the second one wide of the post.

'Nooooooooooo!' Pierre-Emerick groaned. What a waste! He thought back to his old Saint-Étienne manager's best piece of advice: always hit the target.

'That's what Robert would have done,' he thought to himself.

It was just one of those bad days, both for Pierre-Emerick and his team. Isco made it 2–0 and then Cristiano tapped in Real's third. Dortmund had been destroyed.

They did manage to win the home leg, but it wasn't enough to make it through to the Champions League semi-finals again.

'Unlucky, lads,' Klopp told his disappointed players in the dressing room. 'Heads up, we've still got plenty to play for this season!'

In the Bundesliga, Dortmund were a long way behind their big rivals, Bayern Munich. However, if they could beat them away at the Allianz Arena, at least it would give them some confidence ahead of their meeting in the German Cup Final.

'Come on, we can do this!'

Klopp was desperate to win, but he was also planning for the future. Robert had decided to move to Munich, which meant that Dortmund would need a new central striker for next season.

'Auba, that's going to be you!' the manager decided. So, for the big game against Bayern, he left Robert on the bench, and played Pierre-Emerick up front.

'Thanks, boss!' Pierre-Emerick said. He was ready and he couldn't wait to show his team what he could do.

In the twentieth minute, Jonas Hofmann launched a long throw towards Pierre-Emerick, who flicked it on to Marco, who passed it across to Mkhi. *1–0!*

'Great move, guys!' Pierre-Emerick cheered.

The Bayern defence just could not cope with Dortmund's deadly new attack. Mkhi raced forward on the counter-attack and fed the ball to Pierre-Emerick on the right, who squared it to Marco. *2–0!*

'Robert who?' Marco joked as they hugged.

Dortmund would certainly miss their star Polish striker, but Pierre-Emerick had shown that he was ready to step up and play that role instead.

For the German Cup Final, however, Robert was back in the starting line-up. Back on the bench, Pierre-Emerick spent eighty-three long, restless minutes sitting there, waiting for the magic words:

'Auba, you're coming on!'

He raced out onto the field to join the Dortmund attack. They had ten minutes left to score, otherwise the match would go to extra time.

Pierre-Emerick passed to Marco and then sprinted through the middle for the one-two. When he got the ball back, he struck a powerful, first-time shot. For a second, it looked like it was heading into the bottom corner, but in the end, it flew just wide of the post. *So close!*

But Pierre-Emerick didn't stand there with his hands on his head, thinking about 'what if'. Instead, he ran back into position, hoping for another chance, just like Robert had taught him:

'If I do miss one, I just make sure that I score the next one.'

Unfortunately, this time, there was no second chance. In extra time, Bayern won the German Cup again, thanks to goals from Arjen Robben and then Thomas Müller.

The Dortmund players were distraught, but as the days went by, Pierre-Emerick tried to think positively again. Despite the ups and downs, his first season in Germany had been a success overall. Sixteen goals and five assists was a strong start, and he was sure that he would be even better next season.

CHAPTER 18

GOALS, GOALS, GOALS

Pierre-Emerick passed the ball down the line to Łukasz Piszczek and then made a run into the Bayern Munich penalty area. This time, though, it wasn't a super-fast sprint; he was a smart striker these days. If he ran really fast, the defenders would notice him. But if he moved more slowly, maybe he could escape from his marker...

It worked! As the cross came in, Pierre-Emerick was on his own on the edge of the six-yard box. All he had to do was leap into the air and head the ball down into the bottom corner.

Gooooooooooooooooooooooaaaaaaaaaaaaaaaaalllllllllllll llllllllllllll!!!!!!!!!!!!!!!!!!!!

Borussia Dortmund 2 – Bayern Munich 0!

In other words:

Aubameyang 1 – Lewandowski 0!

And Pierre-Emerick had planned an extra special goal celebration for the 2014 German Supercup. He rolled down his right sock and pulled out... a Spiderman mask! When he put it on, the Dortmund fans roared even louder.

Auba! Auba! Auba!

Pierre-Emerick was pleased to win another trophy for Dortmund, but there were others he wanted more: the German Cup, the Bundesliga title, or best of all, the Champions League. That's what he was aiming for now.

But first, he needed to prove himself as Robert's replacement, and Dortmund's new star striker. During the summer, Klopp had signed Adrián Ramos from Hertha Berlin *and* Ciro Immobile from Torino. So as the Bundesliga season started, Pierre-Emerick found himself back out on the right wing. He was still scoring goals, but nowhere near as many as he wanted to.

'I prefer playing through the middle,' he discussed with his dad. 'I'm like Thierry Henry – he started out as a winger too, but then Arsène Wenger turned him into a superstar striker!'

Whenever Pierre-Emerick played up front, he scored goals. He got one against Arsenal and then two against Galatasaray in the Champions League.

'Come on Klopp, Auba's the best striker we've got!' the supporters cried out.

Back in the Bundesliga, Dortmund were really struggling. At the Christmas break in 2014, they were still second from bottom of the league. Something had to change and quickly. By February 2015, Pierre-Emerick had finally done enough to convince Klopp. And once he became Dortmund's centre forward, he didn't look back.

GOALS! Pierre-Emerick scored two – and was involved in all three – in the win over Freiburg.

GOALS! He gave Dortmund the lead against Stuttgart, Schalke and Eintracht Frankfurt.

GOALS! He scored the winners against Mainz and Hannover 96.

Auba to the rescue! With Pierre-Emerick's help, Dortmund bounced all the way back up to seventh place in the Bundesliga. Plus, they made it to the German Cup Final again, beating Bayern Munich in the semis, where Pierre-Emerick faced Robert. After 120 minutes, the match finished Lewandowski 1 – Aubameyang 1. *Time for penalties!*

'I'll take one,' Pierre-Emerick told Klopp confidently, but the shoot-out didn't get that far. Philipp Lahm went first for Bayern. He slipped at the crucial moment and his shot flew high over the bar. İlkay Gündoğan, however, made no mistake. *Advantage to Dortmund!*

'Come on!' Pierre-Emerick muttered, clenching his fist on the halfway line.

Xabi Alonso went second for Bayern, and he slipped too! What was going on? Sebastian Kehl calmly sent the keeper the wrong way. *2–0!*

And that was how it ended. Weidenfeller saved Mario Götze's spot-kick and then Manuel Neuer hit the crossbar. Dortmund were the winners and revenge was so sweet! Pierre-Emerick and his teammates rushed over to hug their goalkeeper hero.

'Right, we *have* to win the final this time!' he shouted as they bounced up and down together.

A cloud of yellow smoke followed the players out onto the pitch in Berlin. It was time for the 2015 German Cup Final – Borussia Dortmund versus Wolfsburg.

There would be interesting battles all over the field – Mkhi against Belgian playmaker Kevin De Bruyne, İlkay Gündoğan against Brazilian midfielder Luiz Gustavo – and Pierre-Emerick against giant Dutch striker, Bas Dost. Both of the latter had scored sixteen goals in the Bundesliga, but Pierre-Emerick had added another eight in the cup competitions. He was just one away from twenty-five for the season…

Dortmund dominated, right from the kick-off. Up front, Pierre-Emerick used his electric pace to chase after everything. He was desperate to make his mark on the final. As Shinji Kagawa got the ball on the right wing, he made a clever run behind

the Wolfsburg centre-back. Naldo didn't notice,
until it was too late...

Shinji spotted Pierre-Emerick's run straight away
and his cross was excellent. Dortmund's star striker
swung out his right leg and volleyed the ball past the
keeper. *1–0!*

*Gooooooooooooooooooooؤaaaaaaaaaaaaaaaalllllllllllll
llllllllllllll!!!!!!!!!!!!!!!!!!!!*

With his arms out wide and a big grin on his face,
Pierre-Emerick was ready to fly. *Ta-da!* He landed the
flip right in front of the delighted Dortmund fans.

Auba! Auba! Auba!

Fame and glory – with big game goals like that,
Pierre-Emerick could achieve both at the same time.

Dortmund had the early lead, but Wolfsburg
fought back fiercely – Gustavo, De Bruyne and Dost
scored three goals in fifteen minutes.

It was 3–1! Pierre-Emerick couldn't believe
what he was watching. Where was the Dortmund
defence?

'Wake up, it's not over yet!' Klopp told them in his
half-time team-talk.

In the second half, Pierre-Emerick tried his best
to get his team back into the game, but it was no
use. At the final whistle in the German Cup Final,
Dortmund were defeated once again. As he trudged
off the field with his runners-up medal, Pierre-
Emerick felt crushed. What was supposed to be
one of the best moments of his whole career had
ended up being one of the worst. Was his team
cursed? Would they ever win a major trophy? It
was so disappointing, but they only had themselves
to blame.

'Come on, let's make sure that we never feel like
this again!' Pierre-Emerick declared, passionately.

No more disappointments; Pierre-Emerick meant
business now. To prove it, he signed a big new
five-year contract with Dortmund – he wasn't going
anywhere! He was excited about working with the
new manager, Thomas Tuchel. They clicked straight
away, and when the new season started, Dortmund's
star striker couldn't stop scoring:

A header against Borussia Mönchengladbach,

A tap-in against Ingolstadt,

Another against Hertha Berlin,
Two penalties against Hannover,
And another against Bayer Leverkusen.

That was six goals in the first five games! Pierre-
Emerick was really living his flashy football dream,
doing funny dances and scoring great goals. If he
scored one more in the next match away at
Hoffenheim, he would break the Bundesliga record.

'No-one has ever started a season like this,' he told
his dad proudly. 'Not even Lewy!'

Could Hoffenheim stop Dortmund's star striker?
No – early in the second half, Gonzalo Castro
chested the ball down in the box and Pierre-Emerick
pounced.

*Goooooooooooooooooooooaaaaaaaaaaaaaaaaallllllllllll
llllllllllllll!!!!!!!!!!!!!!!!!!!*

Pierre-Emerick had taken his scoring to the next
level – the world-class level. Even Robert couldn't
keep up with Gabon's goal machine. He grabbed two
more against Darmstadt and then another against
Bayern. Finally, in the ninth game of the season,

Mainz stopped him from scoring.

Pierre-Emerick's remarkable run was over. But how did he react to going one game without a goal? By scoring another hat-trick in the very next game against Augsburg!

CHAPTER 19

GABON'S GREAT HOPE

Pierre-Emerick was now Dortmund's star striker, as well as Gabon's great hope. His country was really counting on him to lead The Panthers to glory. That was a lot of responsibility for one player, but he never felt the pressure. Pierre-Emerick always played with a smile on his face, because why wouldn't he? He was lucky enough to be living his football dream, and he wanted to make the most of every minute of it.

'It's our job to help bring happiness to the people,' Pierre-Emerick told his international teammate Bruno. 'And so far, we're failing!'

Since reaching the 2012 Africa Cup of Nations quarter-finals, Gabon had gone downhill. They hadn't qualified for the next tournament in 2013, or the 2014 World Cup, despite Pierre-Emerick's hat-trick against Niger.

'Something has to change,' he told himself after a disappointing defeat to Equatorial Guinea.

Although it was very frustrating, Pierre-Emerick refused to give up on glory with Gabon. That penalty miss against Mali still haunted him; he had to try to turn things around. He wanted to become one of the greats of African football, like Didier Drogba and Samuel Eto'o. So in 2015, Pierre-Emerick became the new Panthers captain.

It was a huge honour to lead the national team, just like his dad had done twenty years before him. Pierre-Emerick was determined to do a good job, starting with getting Gabon to the 2015 Africa Cup of Nations.

The Panthers achieved that, no problem, but could they go on and reach the quarter-finals of the tournament again? With Pierre-Emerick wearing the captain's armband, anything was possible.

'Come on, we can win this!' He clapped and

cheered as they kicked off against Burkina Faso.

The Gabon team had definitely improved since 2012, with top new players like Didier Ndong in midfield and Malick Evouna and Frédéric Bulot in attack. However, it was still up to Pierre-Emerick to lead the way.

ZOOM! As soon as the ball was played forward, Pierre-Emerick sprinted between the centre-backs, and into the Burkina Faso box. He tried to poke it past the keeper, but his shot was blocked.

'Ahhhhhhhhhhh!' the Gabon supporters sighed. They expected their star striker to score every time.

But Pierre-Emerick wasn't giving up. As the ball rolled away, he chased after it. He wasn't going to miss a second chance. First, he faked to shoot with his weaker left foot, and then he slid it across to his right. *BANG!* His powerful shot flew into the top corner.

Goooooooooooooooooooooaaaaaaaaaaaaaaaaallllllllllllll lllllllllllll!!!!!!!!!!!!!!!!!!!!

Auba to the rescue! Pierre-Emerick played it cool with his celebration, but on the inside, he was bursting with pride. At the final whistle, Gabon were the winners and the players danced in front of the fans. What a start!

Next up: Congo. In the first half, Gabon created chance after chance, but their shots kept trickling just wide of the post, or rising just over the bar. Sadly, only one of the chances fell to their captain. Pierre-Emerick's free kick swerved through the air, but it was straight at the keeper.

'Ahhhhhhhhhhh!' the Gabon supporters sighed.

'Don't worry, we'll score soon,' their manager Jorge Costa said, but it was Congo who took the lead after some dreadful defending. Gabon tried everything to get the equaliser, but the ball refused to go in.

At full time, Pierre-Emerick was furious. How had they missed so many shots? How had they lost such a winnable game? But it was no use complaining now. As the captain, he needed to lift the team spirit again for the final group game.

'This isn't over yet!' Pierre-Emerick told the other players. 'If we beat Equatorial Guinea, we can still go through. Come on!'

But it was like the Congo match all over again. Gabon wasted chance after chance, and then in the second half, they gave away a silly penalty. When would they learn from their mistakes? Pierre-Emerick could only watch in horror as his dreams of winning the 2015 Africa Cup of Nations were destroyed.

Two years later, however, in 2017 Pierre-Emerick was back to try again. Gabon were the tournament hosts and their leading goalscorer had won the African Footballer of the Year award. Hopes were high – what could possibly go wrong?

Plenty. In the first match against Guinea-Bissau, Pierre-Emerick slid in at the back post to give Gabon the lead.

'Right, we've got to stay focused now!' he warned his teammates as they celebrated together. But in the very last minute, they switched off and Guinea-Bissau grabbed an equaliser. *1–1!* The national stadium in Gabon fell silent.

'Nooooooooooo!' Pierre-Emerick groaned. 'Not again!'

In the next match against Burkina Faso, the Gabon defence were caught out on the counter-attack. Their captain couldn't believe what he was seeing. Why didn't someone clear the ball? Why didn't someone tackle the striker? Why didn't the keeper save the shot? It was all so embarrassing!

Fortunately, fifteen minutes later, Pierre-Emerick got the chance to save The Panthers. *ZOOM!* He sprinted past the Burkina Faso centre-back and got to the ball just before the sliding goalkeeper. *Foul – penalty!*

There was no question about who would take it. This was Pierre-Emerick's opportunity to put things right and make up for that miss in the 2012 shoot-out. As he waited for the referee's whistle, he took a long, deep breath and wiped the sweat from his forehead.

FWEET! He ran up and… sent the keeper the wrong way. *1–1!*

Goooooooooooooooooooooaaaaaaaaaaaaaaaaalllllllllllll llllllllllllll!!!!!!!!!!!!!!!!!!!

There was no time for celebrations. Pierre-Emerick grabbed the ball out of the net and raced back for the restart.

'We can win this!' he urged his teammates along the way.

But Gabon's winning goal just would not arrive. Two games, two disappointing draws. Now, they had no choice but to beat Cameroon, or crash out of their own tournament.

'We can't let our country down!' Pierre-Emerick told his teammates before kick-off.

It turned out to be a match that he would never forget, but sadly, not for the right reasons. One glorious chance could have changed everything. Denis Bouanga raced down the left wing and into the penalty area. Then he crossed the ball to the back post, where Pierre-Emerick was waiting. He had lost his marker, and the empty goal was gaping in front of him.

'Yes, yes, YES!' the Gabon fans were already on their feet, ready to celebrate.

Pierre-Emerick had to score… but he didn't. Somehow, he steered his shot wide of the post.

Everyone was shocked, especially Pierre-Emerick. He lay there on the grass, shaking his head in disbelief.

Gabon did create more chances, but none as good as that one. The match finished 0– 0, and The Panthers were knocked out.

Pierre-Emerick stormed off the pitch, wondering if he would ever play for his country again. What kind of a captain missed a sitter like that? He felt like he had let his people down badly.

But deep down, under all his anger, Pierre-Emerick knew that he would carry on. He could never give up on his beloved Gabon.

CHAPTER 20

ANOTHER TROPHY AT LAST

Back in Germany, Pierre-Emerick was still searching for his first major trophy. Despite his record-breaking start to the 2015–16 season, Robert Lewandowski had beaten him to the Golden Boot, and Bayern had beaten Dortmund in the Bundesliga *and* the German Cup. Again.

'I'm so tired of being second best!' Pierre-Emerick complained to his teammates during preseason training. 'It's time for us to win something!'

'Yeah!' agreed Marco.

'Yeah!' agreed Shinji.

'Yeah!' agreed Sokratis.

Mkhi had moved to Manchester United, but

Tuchel had replaced him with a very talented teenage French forward called Ousmane Dembélé.

'I think he's even faster than you, Auba!' Marco teased.

Pierre-Emerick just laughed. 'No way, that's not possible!'

The three of them together, however, were undoubtedly the new speediest strikeforce in Germany. On the counter-attack, no-one would be able to catch them. So, at the start of the 2016–17 season, Pierre-Emerick set his goals target even higher:

'I scored twenty-five last season, so I'm aiming for thirty this time!'

That was how many Robert had scored during the previous year. Pierre-Emerick was always up for a challenge, especially when it involved his old Dortmund strike partner.

Pierre-Emerick started by scoring two against Mainz, two against Wolfsburg and one against Freiburg.

Auba! Auba! Auba!

Meanwhile, Robert scored three against Werder Bremen, one against Schalke and one against Ingolstadt.

Lewy! Lewy! Lewy!

It was 5–5 after three games each, and their Bundesliga battle went on all season long. By November, it was advantage to Pierre-Emerick. He scored four goals against Hamburg – and then faced Robert's Bayern in *Der Klassiker*.

In the eleventh minute, Pierre-Emerick flicked the ball back to Łukasz Piszczek, who passed out wide to Mario Götze, who crossed it in to... Pierre-Emerick! Thanks to lots of hard work on the training field, he had become the king of the six-yard box. *1–0!*

Goooooooooooooooooooaaaaaaaaaaaaaaaallllllllllll lllllllllllll!!!!!!!!!!!!!!!!!!!

Pierre-Emerick celebrated by doing a few push-ups down on the grass. They were a cheeky tribute to his friend, the French rapper Gradur, who had a famous song about push-ups. He was there in the stadium, but he was supporting Bayern instead!

Auba! Auba! Auba!

As he jogged back to his own half, Pierre-Emerick blew kisses to the delighted Dortmund fans. This was going to be *HIS* season; he was sure of it.

And it wasn't just the Bundesliga defences that had to beware of Dortmund's main man. In the Champions League, Pierre-Emerick scored two goals against his favourite team, Real Madrid, and then three against Benfica.

'You just keep getting better and better!' Tuchel said, giving his star striker a big hug.

At the start of April, Pierre-Emerick and Robert were tied at the top of the Bundesliga scoring chart, with twenty-four goals each. With eight games to go, the race was really on:

Pierre-Emerick scored against Hamburg, then Eintracht Frankfurt, then Borussia Mönchengladbach, then Hoffenheim, and then Augsburg.

Auba! Auba! Auba!

Meanwhile, Robert scored two against Dortmund, two against Wolfsburg and two against RB Leipzig.

Lewy! Lewy! Lewy!

With one game to go, Robert was winning, by thirty goals to twenty-nine.

'You've got to let me score today,' Pierre-Emerick joked with the Dortmund players before their last match against Werder Bremen, 'and as many times as possible!'

Just before half-time, Ousmane chipped a beautiful pass into the Bremen box. Pierre-Emerick watched the ball carefully as it flew over his head and dropped down in front of him. He waited until the perfect moment and then smashed a ferocious volley past the keeper.

Goooooooooooooooooooooaaaaaaaaaaaaaaaaalllllllllllll llllllllllllllll!!!!!!!!!!!!!!!!!!!!!

Goal Number Thirty! With a big grin on his face, Pierre-Emerick held up three fingers on his left hand. One by one, his teammates came over to congratulate him on achieving his target.

'Nice one, Auba!'

'Are you and Lewy going to share the Golden Boot then?'

No way, Pierre-Emerick wanted it all for himself!

In the last few minutes of the match, Dortmund were awarded a penalty. Ousmane grabbed the ball and gave it to Marco, but he passed it on to his strike partner.

'Go on – you take it, Auba!'

If he scored, Dortmund would win the match, and Pierre-Emerick would win the Golden Boot. He stepped up and… sent the keeper the wrong way. *4–3!*

Goooooooooooooooooooaaaaaaaaaaaaaaaaalllllllllllll llllllllllllllll!!!!!!!!!!!!!!!!!!!!

Goal Number Thirty-One! As he raced towards the corner flag, Pierre-Emerick jumped up and punched the air. What a feeling! There were just no words to describe his happiness in that moment.

It was Bayern who won the Bundesliga title yet again, but Dortmund still had the chance to win another trophy at last. They were in another German Cup Final, and this time, they were taking on Eintracht Frankfurt. Could Pierre-Emerick earn a winners' medal to go with his Golden Boot?

He hoped so. Before kick-off in Berlin, Pierre-Emerick did his special handshake with Marco, and then with Ousmane. Together, they were on a mission to bring the trophy back to Dortmund.

'Let's do this!'

At the start of the second half, however, the score was still 1–1, and Marco had to go off with an injury. The pressure was now on Pierre-Emerick to be their main matchwinner.

In a crowded penalty area, Ousmane managed to lift the ball to the back post, where Pierre-Emerick met it with an acrobatic volley. *BANG!* It hit a defender on the goal line and crashed off the crossbar.

So close! It would have been a wonderful way to win the German Cup Final. But Pierre-Emerick picked himself up and carried on...

In the sixty-fifth minute, Christian Pulisic powered into the box and collided with the Frankfurt keeper. *Foul – penalty!*

With Marco off the field, it was Pierre-Emerick's job to take it. He took a long, deep breath, then ran up and... chipped the ball straight down the middle. *2–1!*

Goooooooooooooooooooaaaaaaaaaaaaaaaallllllllllll llllllllllllllll!!!!!!!!!!!!!!!!!!!!

Pierre-Emerick had scored with a Panenka, one of the coolest penalties around.

'Come ooooooooooonnnnnnn!' he roared as he raced over to perform his flip.

Auba! Auba! Auba!

Pierre-Emerick was the Dortmund hero, helping his club to win another German Cup Final at last.

'We did it, we finally did it!' he screamed out again and again as he rushed over to Shinji and Sokratis.

Pierre-Emerick was in the mood to party. Soon, he had a yellow-and-black scarf tied around his head as he laughed and joked around. After lots of hugs, dances and special handshakes, it was time to lift the trophy. As Marcel, their captain, raised it high into the sky, yellow confetti filled the air and the players sang together, loudly and proudly.

Campeones, Campeones, Olé! Olé! Olé!
Lalalalalalalalalala Dortmund!

It was the perfect end to Pierre-Emerick's perfect

season. The Golden Boot and the German Cup made a beautiful pair.

The celebrations went on for days. When their aeroplane arrived back in Dortmund, there were hundreds of fans there to greet them. Then when they paraded the trophy around the city on an open top bus, thousands turned out to wave and cheer. And wearing cool sunglasses and a backwards baseball cap, Pierre-Emerick was, of course, the star of the show.

CHAPTER 21

ARRIVING AT ARSENAL

During his four years at Dortmund, Pierre-Emerick had developed from an inconsistent winger into one of the best strikers in the world. Forty goals in one season – that put him right at the top next to Messi and Ronaldo!

Pierre-Emerick would always be grateful to the club, the fans and his two managers, Klopp and Tuchel, but was it now time to move on? Although he longed to lift the Bundesliga title, Dortmund were still trailing way behind Bayern Munich. How were they going to get any closer when they kept selling their stars every summer? Ousmane was the latest player to leave, joining Messi and Luis Suárez at Barcelona. Hey, what about Pierre-Emerick, the best goalscorer in Germany?

'I think I need a new challenge too,' he admitted to his dad.

'How about signing for Real Madrid?' Yaya suggested. 'That was always your dream as a kid.'

And his grandad's too. Pierre-Emerick had made him a promise before he died: 'One day, Grandpa, I'm going to be a Real striker, just like Hugo Sánchez!'

Pierre-Emerick loved the idea of playing for his favourite football club, but what about Cristiano Ronaldo, and Karim Benzema, and Gareth Bale, and Lucas Vázquez, and Marco Asensio... Surely there wasn't space for *another* striker?

'AC Milan could be an option as well,' Yaya informed him.

Interesting! But would Pierre-Emerick really want to go back to his first professional team, where the youth coaches had called him 'The Boy with the Square Feet' and told him that he wouldn't make it at the top level? Although he had already proved them wrong, perhaps he still had unfinished business in Italy. And AC Milan did desperately need a great new goalscorer…

But as the 2017–18 season began, Pierre-Emerick found himself still at Dortmund. Those big-money moves to Madrid or Milan hadn't happened, after all. Never mind, there was no need to be too disappointed. At twenty-eight, he still had many more years ahead of him. He would just have to stay in Germany until the January transfer window, and then find a new club after that. While he waited, he kept doing what he did best.

GOAL! In the Bundesliga, Pierre-Emerick scored one against Wolfsburg, then two against Köln, and then three against Borussia Mönchengladbach.

GOAL! In the German Cup, he grabbed a hat-trick in his one and only game.

GOAL! In the Champions League, he slid a shot past Tottenham's Hugo Lloris and then chipped the ball over Real Madrid's Keylor Navas.

By the time January arrived, Pierre-Emerick was already on twenty-one goals. Dortmund, however,

were down in sixth place in the Bundesliga and
knocked out of the cup competitions. What a
disaster! Pierre-Emerick was more determined than
ever to move on, but where?

While Real Madrid and AC Milan were making
up their minds, Arsenal swooped in with a big offer
to buy him.

It didn't take much to persuade Pierre-Emerick. He
had always dreamed of becoming 'the new Thierry
Henry', and where better to do that than at Arsenal,
the French striker's old Premier League club? Like
his hero, Pierre-Emerick was super-speedy and scored
lots and lots of goals.

'The Arsenal fans are going to adore you!' the
manager Arsène Wenger assured him.

Pierre-Emerick would also be reunited with an
old friend because Mkhi had just moved there from
Manchester United.

'Come join me!' his old teammate urged. 'You'll
love it here in London!'

Dortmund rejected the first two bids, but on the
last day of the transfer window, a third offer was

finally accepted. At £57 million, Pierre-Emerick was Arsenal's new record signing.

'I'm really happy to be here in this great team,' he said when the big news was announced.

It was a fresh start for Pierre-Emerick, and he couldn't wait to prove himself on the pitch. But first, there was an important question to answer: what number would he wear? At Dortmund, he had always been '17', but that shirt was already taken at Arsenal. '7' instead? No, that now belonged to Mkhi.

'What about Number Fourteen?' Pierre-Emerick suggested.

'Are you sure?'

Number 14 was Henry's old number. Did Pierre-Emerick really want to put even more pressure on himself to perform?

'Yes, I'm sure.'

Even though he was arriving halfway through the season, Pierre-Emerick wasn't going to use that as an excuse. He would just have to adapt to Premier League football as quickly as possible. He was ready to follow in the footsteps of an Arsenal legend like Henry.

Just two days after the transfer was completed, Pierre-Emerick was in the starting line-up against Everton at the Emirates. He had Alex Iwobi to his left, Mkhi to his right, and Mesut Özil and Aaron Ramsey sat just behind.

'Right, let's score some goals!' he called out confidently. He had another cool new haircut for the special occasion.

The first goal arrived after only six minutes. Mesut played a pass into Pierre-Emerick, who cleverly flicked the ball through to Mkhi, who crossed to Aaron. *1–0!*

'Welcome to the team, Auba!' Mkhi shouted as Pierre-Emerick joined the happy Arsenal huddle.

What an instant impact, but was there more to come? The supporters certainly hoped so.

'Shooooot!' they shouted every time he touched the ball.

Pierre-Emerick was determined to score on his Premier League debut, but he sliced his first shot way wide of the post. Then he watched as his teammate Laurent Koscielny dived in front of him to score Arsenal's second goal.

'Keep going,' he told himself. All he needed was one good pass and his pace would do the rest…

When Nacho Monreal played a long pass down the left wing, *ZOOM!* Pierre-Emerick was off. This was it – his big chance. He beat the Everton defenders to the ball and then dribbled into the penalty area.

Shooooot!

On his weaker left foot, Pierre-Emerick fired a shot goalwards, but Jordan Pickford threw himself down and saved it with his legs.

'Unlucky, Auba!' the Arsenal fans clapped and cheered encouragingly.

Pierre-Emerick pulled up his socks and carried on. He didn't miss many; it was only a matter of time before he scored…

Alex passed to Mkhi, who spun and played it swiftly through to Pierre-Emerick.

'Offside!' the Everton defenders cried out desperately, but the flag stayed down. He was too quick for even the linesman to see.

Pierre-Emerick was now one-on-one with Pickford,

who was rushing out towards him. He *had* to score
this time. He waited for the keeper to dive down and
then at the crucial moment, he chipped the ball over
his outstretched arm and into the net. *4–0!*

*Goooooooooooooooooooaaaaaaaaaaaaaaaaalllllllllllll
lllllllllllllll!!!!!!!!!!!!!!!!!!!*

He had scored with a world-class finish on his
Arsenal debut, and the crowd went absolutely
wild. Wherever he went, he brought goals and
entertainment with him.

'Thanks, Mkhi!' Pierre-Emerick called out,
pointing and grinning at his friend.

As he stood there in front of the fans, he felt on top
of the world. He had the fame and he had the glory
too. There was no stopping him at his new club.

GOAL! Pierre-Emerick pulled one back against
Brighton.

GOAL! Pierre-Emerick and Mkhi set each other up
in the 3–0 win over Watford.

GOAL! Pierre-Emerick scored twice against Stoke
City.

What a start – Pierre-Emerick was taking the

Premier League by storm! He was breaking records already, just like he did at Dortmund. With his second goal against Stoke, he became the first Arsenal player to ever score five times in his first six games at the club.

'I love this league and this league loves me!' Pierre-Emerick laughed with Mkhi and Mesut.

Even losing to Manchester City in the League Cup final didn't stop him from enjoying life in England. Never mind, there was always next year! Pierre-Emerick was pleased with his first half-season at Arsenal. In no time at all, he had found his scoring form. Nine goals in thirteen games was a terrific total, and there was still one more match to go. It was a very important one too. After twenty-two years at Arsenal, this would be Wenger's last match as manager.

'Come on lads, we have to say goodbye with a win!' Aaron declared in the dressing room before kick-off.

'Yeah!' cheered Pierre-Emerick together with his teammates.

For most of the first half, however, Huddersfield Town were the better side. They created lots of chances, but they just couldn't score a goal. That's what Pierre-Emerick was there to do for Arsenal.

Alexandre Lacazette swapped passes with Mkhi and then poked the ball through to Aaron. His shot looked like it might be going in, but Pierre-Emerick slid in to make 100 per cent sure. *1–0!*

Goooooooooooooooooooooaaaaaaaaaaaaaaaaallllllllllll llllllllllllllll!!!!!!!!!!!!!!!!!!!!!

Thanks to Pierre-Emerick, Wenger got the winning end that he deserved. The Arsenal players were sad to see their manager leave, but at the same time, they were also excited for the future.

'Just you wait until I play a whole Premier League season,' Pierre-Emerick boldly predicted. 'I'm going for the Golden Boot next year!'

CHAPTER 22

LOVING LIFE WITH LACA

From just inside the Cardiff City half, Mesut played a pass through to Alexandre. He had his back to goal, but the Arsenal forward knew exactly what to do next.

With the outside of his right foot, he flicked the ball on, into his strike partner's path. Pierre-Emerick took one touch to control it and then curled a shot into the bottom corner. *2–1!*

Gooooooooooooooooooooaaaaaaaaaaaaaaaaalllllllllllll llllllllllllllll!!!!!!!!!!!!!!!!!!

Pierre-Emerick pointed at Alexandre, and Alexandre pointed at Pierre-Emerick. Then they began to dance together.

Yes, Pierre-Emerick knew Mkhi and Sokratis well from their Dortmund days, but 'Auba' and 'Laca' were Arsenal's new BFFs. Although Pierre-Emerick was two years older, they had lots in common: their younger years in France, goals, music and, of course, a desire to entertain. They even had their own special brand of goal celebration. When Laca scored a late winner against Cardiff, Auba raced over to him. With one arm behind their backs, they bowed and shook hands like old-fashioned gentlemen.

'Well done, sir!'

The Arsenal fans loved to see their star strikers having so much fun together. They were becoming one of the deadliest duos in the Premier League.

Against Everton, Laca scored the first and Auba scored the second. *2–0!*

Against Fulham, Laca scored twice and so did Auba. *5–1!*

With their forwards on fire, Arsenal won seven Premier League games in a row. They moved up into the Top Four.

'We're back where we belong!' Héctor Bellerín
cheered.

If they could keep it up, The Gunners could qualify
for the Champions League again. That was the main
aim, especially for Pierre-Emerick. He had already
shown at Dortmund that he was talented enough
to shine at the top level. Now, with Laca, Mkhi and
Mesut at Arsenal, he believed he could shine even
brighter in Europe.

But that was still a long way off. Pierre-Emerick
was taking things one game and one goal at a time.
For now, he was focused on helping Arsenal beat
their big local rivals, Tottenham. In his only previous
North London derby, his team had lost 1–0 away
at Wembley.

This time, though, Arsenal were at home at the
Emirates, so defeat just wasn't an option. Pierre-
Emerick couldn't wait for the big game to begin.
Auba and Laca would be up against Harry Kane and
Son Heung-min. With those four guys on the same
pitch, there would surely be plenty of goals!

When Arsenal's Unai Emery announced his team,

however, Alexandre was only on the bench. Pierre-Emerick would be up front on his own, at least for the first half. No problem – he wasn't nervous at all. In fact, as he ran out to warm up, he waved to the Arsenal fans like normal, with a big smile on his face. Derby games like this was what being a professional footballer was all about.

'I'm ready to be the hero!' he thought to himself.

Early on, Pierre-Emerick pounced on Serge Aurier's mistake. And as the Spurs defender tried to win the ball back, he fouled Arsenal's star striker. *Free kick!*

Granit Xhaka curled the ball into the box, but Jan Vertonghen cleared it away with his head. No wait, it wasn't his head; it was his arm!

'Handball!' Pierre-Emerick cried out straight away. He had a perfect view and so did the referee.

Penalty!

Pierre-Emerick grabbed the ball, placed it down on the spot and then took a long, deep breath. He wasn't going to rush this glorious chance to give Arsenal the lead.

Hugo Lloris did his best to put Pierre-Emerick off, but it didn't work. The striker fixed his eyes on the bottom right corner but fired his shot bottom left. *1–0!*

Gooooooooooooooooooooaaaaaaaaaaaaaaaalllllllllllll lllllllllllllll!!!!!!!!!!!!!!!!!!

Pierre-Emerick flipped through the air and landed on his feet in front of the fans. *Ta-da!* Even in the North London derby, he was still the ultimate entertainer.

By half-time, however, Tottenham were winning 2–1. It was time for Arsenal's attacking dream team: Auba and Laca.

'Come on, let's do this!' they cheered together.

In the second half, it was all Arsenal. Héctor played a great pass through to Aaron, who guided it across to Pierre-Emerick on the edge of the Tottenham penalty area. Aurier was closing in to make the tackle, so he had to take the shot early. *BANG!* The ball was in the back of the net before Lloris could even react. *2–2!*

Gooooooooooooooooooooaaaaaaaaaaaaaaaalllllllllllll lllllllllllllll!!!!!!!!!!!!!!!!!!

Pierre-Emerick punched the air with passion and joy. What a fantastic finish – and in the North London derby!

Twenty minutes later, it was Alexandre's turn. Even with three Tottenham defenders surrounding him, he somehow still found the bottom corner. *3–2 to Arsenal!*

Laca to the rescue! He celebrated with a knee-slide, then high-fives, and finally a handshake with Auba.

'Well done, sir!'

And the Auba and Laca show still wasn't over. Pierre-Emerick slipped a beautiful pass through the Spurs defence to set up Lucas Torreira to score. *4–2!*

After the final whistle, the Arsenal players partied on the pitch. Why not? They had beaten their big local rivals in style! As they did a lap of honour around the field, young midfielder Mattéo Guendouzi grabbed Pierre-Emerick's right boot, kissed it and held it up for the crowd like a trophy.

'Hey, let go, Mattéo!' he shouted as he hopped around on one leg.

The Arsenal supporters cheered, thinking it was another new Auba dance.

By Christmas, Pierre-Emerick was one of the league's top scorers with thirteen goals, while Alexandre had six goals and six assists. Whenever they played together, Arsenal were always so exciting to watch.

Auba and Laca scored one each against Fulham on New Year's Day. *4–1!*

Laca gave Arsenal the lead against Chelsea. *2–0!*

Auba scored one against Cardiff and then set one up for his strike partner. *2–1!*

But it wasn't just the two of them; it was all of Arsenal's amazing attackers together. When they played their best, flowing football, they were simply unstoppable.

Mesut scored first against Bournemouth,

Then Mkhi,

Then Pierre-Emerick,

And Alexandre finished it off with a beautiful free kick. *5–1!*

By then, Pierre-Emerick had been taken off, but

he jumped up off the bench to celebrate his friend's great goal. As he stood there on the sideline, he couldn't believe what he saw. Laca was doing his handshake with someone else: Mesut!

'Hey, you can't just replace me like that!' Auba joked.

He was right; Pierre-Emerick was totally irreplaceable, especially during the final months of the 2018–19 season, as Arsenal went in search of silverware.

CHAPTER 23

GUNNING FOR GLORY

When the players walked out at Wembley for the second North London derby of the season, Arsenal were in fourth place in the Premier League – just one point ahead of Manchester United, and three ahead of Chelsea. The Gunners were where they wanted to be, but they couldn't get too comfortable.

'Don't let this slip!' Emery told his team before kick-off.

Away from home against a top team like Tottenham, the Arsenal manager decided that playing Auba and Laca together would be too attacking. So instead, Alexandre started for the first fifty-five minutes and Pierre-Emerick replaced him for the final thirty-five.

As Auba ran onto the field, Arsenal were 1–0 up, thanks to Aaron's goal from Laca's assist. Could they hold on for another famous derby victory? Tottenham pushed forward, looking for the equaliser. Meanwhile, Pierre-Emerick waited for the chance to show off his super-speed in a quick counter-attack. All he needed was one good pass…

But before it arrived, Tottenham were awarded a penalty for a foul on Harry Kane. *1–1!*

A draw wouldn't be too disappointing for Arsenal, but a win would, of course, be even better. In the eighty-eighth minute, Mkhi dribbled forward and delivered the pass that Pierre-Emerick was looking for. He was onto it in a flash, and as he went to dribble past Davinson Sánchez, the Tottenham defender tripped him. *Penalty!*

Pierre-Emerick had the chance to win the game. He had already been an Arsenal hero in one North London derby – could he do it again? He looked confident as he ran up to take it, but so did Lloris in on his goal line. The keeper waited until the last second to dive down low to his right. *SAVED!*

Pierre-Emerick nearly scored the rebound, but Vertonghen got back just in time to make a brave block.

'Noooooooooooo!' Auba groaned. It was a huge opportunity wasted.

Oh well, what was it that Robert had told him during their time together at Dortmund? 'If I do miss one, I just make sure that I score the next one.'

A week later against Manchester United, Arsenal were 1–0 up when Fred fouled Alexandre in the box. *Another penalty!*

Would Pierre-Emerick want to take it after his North London derby failure? Of course! His nerves were as strong as steel, and he needed to make up for his mistake. He stepped up to the spot and… sent David de Gea the wrong way. *2–0!*

Goooooooooooooooooooooaaaaaaaaaaaaaaaalllllllllllll llllllllllllll!!!!!!!!!!!!!!!!!!!

'That's more like it, Auba!' Laca cheered.

Arsenal were still in fourth place after the win

over Manchester United, and were still fighting hard
for that last Champions League place. However,
that wasn't the only thing on the players' minds.
The Gunners were also in the last 16 of the Europa
League. There was a chance that they could still
finish the season with a major trophy.

The away leg against Rennes had been a total
disaster, but Arsenal could still turn things around at
the Emirates. They needed to score at least three goals
and Pierre-Emerick was determined to deliver them.

He got on the end of Aaron's pass and poked the
ball past the keeper. *1–0!*

He chipped a cross to the back post, where Ainsley
Maitland-Niles headed it in. *2–0!*

'Come on, we just need one more now!' Emery
urged his players at half-time.

Arsenal were full of belief. After all, they had
one of the greatest goalscorers in the world. Pierre-
Emerick played a short pass to Mkhi and then
sprinted between the Rennes centre-backs.

'Now!' he shouted, pointing at the space in front
of him.

But instead, Mkhi played it to Sead Kolašinac on the left wing. He fizzed the ball across the six-yard box, past one defender and then another, until it fell to… Pierre-Emerick. Like all great goalscorers, he was in the right place at the right time, and he couldn't miss. *3–0!*

Goooooooooooooooooooaaaaaaaaaaaaaaaalllllllllll llllllllllllll!!!!!!!!!!!!!!!!!!

Arsenal were through to the Europa League quarter-finals! Pierre-Emerick ran over to the advertising boards behind the goal to collect a special costume for his celebration – a Black Panther mask! Forget Spiderman, this was his new favourite superhero film. With the mask on, Pierre-Emerick crossed his arms like an 'X' in the classic Black Panther pose.

'Super-Auba saves the day!' Mattéo joked.

Arsenal cruised past Napoli in the quarters to set up a semi-final against Valencia. The Spaniards took the lead in the first leg at the Emirates, but after that, it became the Auba and Laca Show.

Alexandre used his strength to escape from his

marker and then played a beautiful pass between
the centre-backs. *ZOOM!* Pierre-Emerick raced onto
it and dribbled into the penalty area. What next – a
shot? No, as he looked up, he spotted his strike
partner's run. Alexandre was all on his own in the
middle with an empty goal to aim for. *1–1!*

'Thanks, Auba!'

'Hey, what are best friends for?'

The first leg finished 3–1 to Arsenal – two goals
from Alexandre and one from Pierre-Emerick. The
second leg, however, was all about Auba.

From Alexandre's flick-on, Pierre-Emerick chested
the ball down before firing a lovely, looping shot into
the bottom corner.

*Goooooooooooooooooooooaaaaaaaaaaaaaaaalllllllllllll
llllllllllllll!!!!!!!!!!!!!!!!!!!*

'Thanks, Laca!'

'Hey, what are best friends for?'

Alexandre scored a second goal and Pierre-
Emerick scored a third. Right, he thought, he had
twenty-five minutes to complete his first-ever Arsenal
hat-trick...

The game was effectively already over, but not for Pierre-Emerick. He kept moving into space and calling for the ball. He dummied Mattéo's pass, letting it run through to Mkhi. *ZOOM!* Pierre-Emerick burst into the box and collected Mkhi's through-ball. The angle was quite tight for a shot, but there was no-one waiting in the middle. Plus, he was on a hat-trick!

Pierre-Emerick steadied himself and then blasted the ball into the roof of the net. The Valencia keeper just stood there, frozen in shock.

Gooooooooooooooooooooaaaaaaaaaaaaaaaaalllllllllllll llllllllllllll!!!!!!!!!!!!!!!!!!

Pierre-Emerick got hat-trick hugs from Mattéo, and Mkhi, and Laca, and Sokratis, and Ainsley. It felt so good to be the superstar.

'Auba, you're amazing!'

'I hope you've got something special up your sleeve for the final!'

Before the final, a big day in Baku, Azerbaijan, Arsenal had one last Premier League game to go. Sadly, fourth place had slipped out of their grasp, after defeats to Crystal Palace, Wolves and Leicester City.

Pierre-Emerick still had something to play for, however. With twenty goals, he was joint second in the race for the Golden Boot, level with Sadio Mané and Sergio Agüero, and two behind Mohamed Salah. So, how many could he score on the last day against Burnley?

Two! In the end, three amazing Africans were tied at the top on twenty-two goals: Salah, Mané and Auba. They had to share the Golden Boot, although they each got a glittering trophy of their own.

Pierre-Emerick was very proud of his goalscoring achievements, but a team trophy was what he wanted most of all. So far, he only had two German Super Cups and two League Cups to show for his eleven seasons as a professional footballer. That was nowhere near enough.

The Europa League trophy would be an excellent addition to the collection. To win it, Arsenal would need to beat their London rivals Chelsea in the final. It wouldn't be easy, but with Auba and Laca up front, anything was possible.

It was the biggest game of Pierre-Emerick's career, and his chance to show what a world-class striker he was. These were the matches that mattered most, that helped turn a star into a *super*star. Arsenal were counting on him.

In the seventeenth minute, Pierre-Emerick flicked a clever header into Alexandre's path. He was too quick for César Azpilicueta, but what about the Chelsea keeper, who was rushing out of his goal? Alexandre got to the ball just before Kepa, but as he tried to dribble around him, he felt that he was fouled.

'Penalty!' Alexandre and Pierre-Emerick cried out together.

But after checking with VAR, the referee said no. Never mind, Arsenal would just need to find another way to win.

Pierre-Emerick did his best to get into the game, but he was a goalscorer, not a playmaker. His manager didn't want him dropping deep to pick up the ball; he wanted him right up top, ready to race towards goal when the pass was played. But that day, the killer pass never arrived for Pierre-Emerick. He only had four shots, and not one of them hit the target.

At the other end, Chelsea struck with four second-half goals. And to make matter worse, the last came from an error from Pierre-Emerick. He lost the ball in his own half and Eden Hazard took full advantage.

'Nooooooooo!' Pierre-Emerick groaned. His dream of being Arsenal's Europa League Final hero had turned into a nightmare, and all he could do was watch and wait for the final whistle to blow.

It was one of the lowest points in Pierre-Emerick's football life, but nothing could keep him down for long. He was a positive, happy kind of guy. After a relaxing holiday back home in Laval, he would bounce back stronger; he always did.

Once the disappointment faded, Pierre-Emerick was able to look back proudly on a superb season: thirty-one goals, eight assists, a Europa League runners-up medal and a shared Golden Boot. Not bad for 'The Boy with the Square Feet'.

Pierre-Emerick had come so far since those tough, early years at AC Milan and those frustrating times on loan in France. He hadn't let anything get in the way of his flashy football dream, and with lots of hard work, he had achieved it. At Saint-Étienne, Pierre-Emerick finally developed the super-shooting to go with his super-speed. Then at Borussia Dortmund, he went on to become one of the greatest goalscorers in Germany, and even in the world.

And now? Pierre-Emerick was off to an excellent start at Arsenal, but there was surely still plenty more to come. More goals, more celebrations, more fame and more glory.

Turn the page for a sneak preview of
another brilliant football story by
Matt and Tom Oldfield. . .

MBAPPE

Available now!

CHAPTER 1

FROM RUSSIA WITH LOVE

On 14 July 2018, Kylian sent a message to his millions of social media followers, from Russia with love: 'Happy French national day everyone. Let's hope the party continues until tomorrow night!'

'Tomorrow night' – 15 July – the French national team would be playing in the World Cup final at the Luzhniki Stadium in Moscow. It was the most important football match on the planet and Kylian's country was counting on him.

So far, he hadn't let them down at all. In fact, Kylian had been France's speedy superstar, scoring the winning goal against Denmark, and then two more in an amazing man-of-the-match performance against Argentina. That all made him the nation's best 'Number 10' since Zinedine Zidane back in 1998.

That was the year that France last won the World Cup.

That was also the year that Kylian was born.

Thanks to their new young superstar, '*Les Bleus*' were now the favourites to lift the famous golden trophy again. They had already beaten Lionel Messi's Argentina, Luis Suárez's Uruguay in the quarter-finals, and Eden Hazard's Belgium in the semi-finals. Now, the only nation standing in their way was Luka Modrić's Croatia.

'You've done so well to get this far,' the France manager, Didier Deschamps, told them as kick-off approached and the nerves began to jangle. 'Now, you just need to go out there and finish off the job!'

A massive 'Yeah!' echoed around the room. It was one big team effort, from captain Hugo Lloris in goal through to Kylian, Antoine Griezmann and Olivier Giroud in attack. Everyone worked hard and everyone worked together.

By the way, those jangling nerves didn't belong to Kylian. No way, he was the coolest character around! He never let anything faze him. When he was younger, he hadn't just hoped to play in a World Cup final; he had expected it. It was all part of his killer plan to conquer the football world.

Out on the pitch for the final in Moscow, Kylian sang the words of the French national anthem with a big smile on his face. As a four-year-old, some people had laughed at his ambitious dreams. Well, they definitely weren't laughing now.

'Right, let's do this!' Paul Pogba clapped and cheered as they took up their positions. His partnership with Kylian would be key for France. Whenever Paul got the ball in midfield, he would look to find his pacy teammate with a perfect pass.

Kylian's first action of the final, however, was in defence. He rushed back quickly to block a Croatia cross.

'Well done!' France's centre-back Samuel Umtiti shouted.

Once that was done, it was all about attacking. Even in a World Cup final, Kylian wasn't afraid to try his tricks and flicks. They didn't always work but it was worth the risk.

It was an end-to-end first half, full of exciting action. First, Antoine curled in a dangerous free kick and Mario Mandžukić headed the ball into his own net. 1–0 to France! Kylian punched the air – what a start!

Ivan Perišić equalised for Croatia but then he handballed it in his own box. Penalty! Antoine stepped up... and scored – 2–1 to France!

The players were happy to hear the half-time whistle blow. They needed a break to breathe and regroup. Although France were winning, they still had work to do if they wanted to become World Champions again.

'We need to calm things down and take control of the game,' Deschamps told his players. 'Stay smart out there!'

Kylian listened carefully to his manager's message. He needed to relax and play to his strengths – his skill but also his speed. This was his chance to go down in World Cup history:

Pelé in 1958,

Diego Maradona in 1986,

Zidane in 1998,

Ronaldo in 2002,

Kylian in 2018?

In the second half, France's superstars shone much more brightly. Kylian collected Paul's long pass and sprinted straight past the Croatia centre-back. Was he about to score in his first World Cup final? No, the keeper came out to make a good save.

'Ohhhh!' the supporters groaned in disappointment.

But a few minutes later, Paul and Kylian linked up again. From wide on the right wing, Kylian dribbled towards goal. Uh oh, the Croatia left-back was in big trouble.

With a stepover and a little hop, Kylian cut inside towards goal but in a flash, he fooled the defender with another quick change of direction.

'Go on!' the France fans urged their exciting young hero.

What next? Kylian still had two defenders in front of him, so he pulled it back to Antoine instead. He couldn't find a way through either so he passed it on to Paul. Paul's first shot was blocked but his second flew into the bottom corner. 3–1!

Kylian threw his arms up in the air and then ran over to congratulate his friend. Surely, France had one hand on the World Cup trophy now.

Antoine had scored, and so had Paul. That meant it must be Kylian's turn next! He would have to score soon, however, in case Deschamps decided to take him off early...

When he received the pass from Lucas Hernández, Kylian was in the middle of the pitch, at least ten yards outside the penalty area. Was he too far out to shoot? No, there was no such thing as 'too far' for Kylian! He shifted the ball to the right and then BANG! He tucked the ball into the bottom corner before the keeper could even dive. 4–1!

Goooooooooooooooooooaaaaaaaaaaaaaaaalllllllllll llllllllllllll!!!!!!!!!!!!!!!!!

As his teammates rushed over to him, Kylian had

just enough time for his trademark celebration. With a little jump, he planted his feet, folded his arms across his chest, and tried to look as cool as he could. That last part was really hard because he had just scored in a World Cup final!

The next thirty minutes ticked by very slowly but eventually, the game was over. France 4 Croatia 2 – they were the 2018 World Champions!

Allez Les Bleus! Allez Les Bleus! Allez Les Bleus!

Kylian used the last of his energy to race around the pitch, handing out hugs to everyone he saw: his sad opponents, his happy teammates, his manager, EVERYONE! In that amazing moment, he would have hugged every single French person in the world if he could. Instead, he blew kisses at the cameras. From Russia with love!

And Kylian's incredible night wasn't over yet. Wearing his country's flag around his waist, he walked up on stage to collect the tournament's Best Young Player award from Emmanuel Macron.

'Thank you, you're a national hero now!' the French President told him proudly.

'My pleasure, Sir!' Kylian replied.

Would his smile ever fade? Certainly not while he had a World Cup winners' medal around his neck and the beautiful World Cup trophy in his hands. He didn't ever want to let go. Kylian kissed it and raised it high into the Moscow night sky.

'Hurray!' the fans cheered for him.

At the age of nineteen, Kylian was already living out his wildest dreams. The boy from Bondy had become a World Cup winner and football's next great superstar.

AUBAMEYANG HONOURS

Saint-Étienne
🏆 Coupe de la Ligue: 2012–13

Borussia Dortmund
🏆 DFB-Pokal: 2016–17
🏆 DFL Supercup: 2013, 2014

Individual
🏆 Ligue 1 Best African Player: 2012–13
🏆 Ligue 1 Team of the Year: 2012–13
🏆 CAF Team of the Year: 2013, 2014, 2015, 2016, 2018
🏆 Borussia Dortmund Player of the Season: 2014–15

🏆 African Footballer of the Year: 2015
🏆 Bundesliga Player of the Year: 2015–16
🏆 Bundesliga Team of the Year: 2016–17
🏆 Bundesliga Top Goalscorer: 2016–17
🏆 Premier League Golden Boot: 2018–19

AUBAMEYANG

14

THE FACTS

NAME: Pierre-Emerick Emiliano François Aubameyang

DATE OF BIRTH: 18 June 1989

AGE: 30

PLACE OF BIRTH: Laval, France

NATIONALITY: Gabonese

BEST FRIEND: Alexandre Lacazette

CURRENT CLUB: Arsenal

POSITION: ST

THE STATS

Height (cm):	185
Club appearances:	463
Club goals:	238
Club trophies:	4
International appearances:	59
International goals:	24
International trophies:	0
Ballon d'Ors:	0

★ ★ ★ **HERO RATING: 87** ★ ★ ★

GREATEST MOMENTS

27 JANUARY 2012, GABON 3–2 MOROCCO

After scoring on his Gabon debut in 2009, Pierre-Emerick led his country to the 2012 Africa Cup of Nations. With three goals in three games, he shot The Panthers to the quarter-finals, following in his father's footsteps. The pick of Pierre-Emerick's strikes was this vicious volley against Morocco.

20 APRIL 2013, SAINT-ÉTIENNE 1–0 RENNES

In his first-ever cup final, Pierre-Emerick produced
a moment of magic to lead Saint-Étienne to victory.
It wasn't a super shot this time, though; it was a
curling cross with the outside of his right foot to set up
Brandão. Pierre-Emerick ended his breakthrough season
with a well-earned trophy.

27 MAY 2017, EINTRACHT FRANKFURT 1–2 BORUSSIA DORTMUND

This was the day when Pierre-Emerick finally lifted a
major trophy at Dortmund. After losing three German
Cup finals in a row, they won it at last, thanks to
Auba's cheeky Panenka penalty. It was the perfect way
to end his best-ever scoring season.

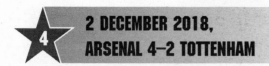

2 DECEMBER 2018,
ARSENAL 4–2 TOTTENHAM

In only his second North London derby, Pierre-Emerick starred in a famous Arsenal victory. He opened the scoring from the penalty spot, and then started the second-half comeback with a beautiful first-time finish. To cap it all off, he set up Lucas Torreira for the fourth goal.

9 MAY 2019,
VALENCIA 2–4 ARSENAL

The Europa League Final didn't go according to plan for Pierre-Emerick and Arsenal, but the semi-final second leg sure did. Teaming up with Laca again, he scored his first-ever hat-trick for The Gunners. The Valencia defence just could not cope with Pierre-Emerick's super-speed and super-shooting.

PLAY LIKE YOUR HEROES

AUBA'S SOMERSAULT
CELEBRATION

STEP 1: First, you'll need to score a goal, and a great one if possible. Try an acrobatic volley or an overhead kick if you dare!

STEP 2: GOAL! After making sure that the ball has crossed the line, turn away and head towards your fans near the corner flag.

STEP 3: Make every movement look as cool as you can. So, don't sprint – jog. And don't show your excitement; stay calm like you score great goals all the time.

STEP 4: When you're ready, spring up off the grass and FLIP!

STEP 5: As you land on your feet, put your hands down to steady yourself. Then jump up, look out at the crowd, and throw your arms out wide like a true entertainer. *Ta-da!*

TEST YOUR KNOWLEDGE

QUESTIONS

1. What position did Pierre-Emerick's dad play?

2. Which club did Pierre-Emerick support as a kid and why?

3. Other than his dad, name at least two of Pierre-Emerick's childhood football heroes.

4. How old was Pierre-Emerick when he joined AC Milan?

5. Which four French clubs did Pierre-Emerick play for on loan?

6. Which four countries did Pierre-Emerick have to choose between at international level?

7. Pierre-Emerick scored on his Dortmund debut – true or false?

8. Which striker did Pierre-Emerick play alongside and then compete against in Germany?

9. What shirt number did Pierre-Emerick choose to wear at Arsenal and why?

10. Which two former Dortmund teammates does Pierre-Emerick play with at Arsenal?

11. Which two Liverpool stars shared the 2018–19 Premier League Golden Boot with Pierre-Emerick?

Answers below. . . No cheating!

1. *Defensive midfield* 2. *Real Madrid, because his Spanish grandad was a big fan* 3. *Any of Hugo Sánchez, George Weah, Thierry Henry and Sokratis* 4. *17* 5. *Dijon, Lille, Monaco and Saint-Étienne* 6. *France, Spain, Gabon and Italy* 7. *False, but he did score a hat-trick in his first Bundesliga game!* 8. *Robert Lewandowski* 9. *14, because 17 and 7 were taken and because it was Thierry Henry's old number* 10. *Henrikh and Sokratis* 11. *Mohamed Salah and Sadio Mané*